MW00390093

Glass Animals
of the Depression Era

Lee Garmon
and
Dick Spencer

COLLECTOR BOOKS
A Division of Schroeder Publishing Co., Inc.

The current values in this book should be used only as a guide. They are not intended to set prices, which vary from one section of the country to another. Auction prices as well as dealer prices vary greatly and are affected by condition as well as demand. Neither the Authors nor the Publisher assumes responsibility for any losses that might be incurred as a result of consulting this guide.

Searching For A Publisher?

We are always looking for knowledgeable people considered to be experts within their fields. If you feel that there is a real need for a book on your collectible subject and have a large comprehensive collection, contact us.

COLLECTOR BOOKS
P.O. Box 3009
Paducah, Kentucky 42002-3009

Cover Photos:

Middle left: Tiffin, see page 185.
Lower left: Heisey, see page 92.
Upper right: New Martinsville, see page 165.
Middle right: Paden City, see page 168.
Lower right: Cambridge Glass Co., see page 24.

Back cover: Viking, see page 195.

Additional copies of this book may be ordered from:

COLLECTOR BOOKS
P.O. Box 3009
Paducah, Kentucky 42002-3009

or

Lee Garmon
1529 Whittier Street
Springfield, IL 62704

Dick Spencer
1203 N. Yale
O'Fallon, IL 62269

@ $19.95 each. Add $2.00 for postage and handling.

Copyright: Lee Garmon, Dick Spencer, 1993.

This book or any part thereof may not be reproduced without the written consent of the Authors and Publisher.

1 2 3 4 5 6 7 8 9 0

This Book is Dedicated To

Dwight Garmon
and
Pat Spencer

Our partners in life, who helped make this happen!

Acknowledgments and Appreciation

Our sincere thanks go out to those who gave of their time and effort, through loaning prized pieces for photography, supplying needed information, helping with pricing, and just letting us lean!

A very special thanks to Neil and Eddie Unger who went the distance.

Fred Bickenheuser – Tiffin
P.J. Rosso, Jr. and Lorraine Kovar – Westmoreland
Bill and Phyllis Smith – Cambridge
Addie and Everett Miller – New Martinsville
Milbra Long – Fostoria
Bob and Sharon Huxford
Dick Green
Gene Florence
Gail Krause – Duncan & Miller

Ferril J. Rice – Fenton
Wanda Huffman
Mary Van Pelt
J.W. Courter – Aladdin Lamps
Lynn Welker
Frank Wollenhaupt
Louise Ream
Antique Publications

Shared Collections:

Verna and Emil Boucher
Jerry and Carrie Domitz
Rita Lesko
Jan Cimarossa
Pat and Paul Randolph
Willie Kulick
Linda Bogan
Vern Garrett
Floyd Craft
Doris Frizzell's Research Library
Alray Zipfel
Ed Pitts
Jewell Gowan

John and Judy Bine
Charles Larson
Beth Finkle
Harold and Mildred Willey
John Day
Jean Day
Ron Morgan
Dick Marsh
Chuck Bails
Boyd Art Glass
Bob & Myrna Garrison
Marilyn Kreutz

Thanks also to Tom Clouser of Curtis and Mays Studio, Paducah, Kentucky, and to Jane White, Lisa Stroup, and the entire staff at Collector Books.

Table of Contents

Introduction

This book is basically a compilation of solid glass animal figurines and figural flower holders of the Depression Era; however, for the readers pleasure we included some closely related items, because of their rarity, that do not fall into either of the foregoing categories. Extensive research turned up information on these related pieces and we felt obligated to picture them and share the information with the collector. Research continues to be a fascinating learning experience, at times revealing new truths, which contradict long accepted conclusions. We have presented in this publication all new information we discovered regarding the subject material.

We fully realize that most glass swans are not solid glass animals but they have been accepted by dealers and collectors alike as "glass animals," therefore, we have included them in this book.

Over the years, as many glass companies closed their doors, the molds have been scattered and sometimes destroyed, especially during the war effort in the 1940's. We have tried to account for as many molds as possible, primarily through identification of companies making reissues from the original molds. Whenever possible we have included production dates on both original and reissues.

It would be premature, at this time, to price current reissues made from molds which were active during the Depression Era under their original owners. A secondary market on these reissues is yet to be firmly established.

Measurements reflected for items shown in this publication are actual measurements made by the authors. One must remember when dealing with handmade glass, especially items which have been finished by grinding and polishing, the measurements will vary.

The efforts and labor expended in writing this book is an expression of our love for Glass Animals and Figural Flower Holders.

Enjoy!

Pricing

Values reflected in this book should be used only as a guide. We are not attempting to establish prices on items shown. Prices are normally established by supply and demand; however, they will vary from dealer to dealer and are influenced by condition of item, various regions of the country, auctions, and by individuals selling items without knowledge as to their true value. Items being reissued are priced by their producer. One often hears from sellers that book prices are too low, however, you hear from buyers that book prices are too high. Some items in this book are from private collections and the owners ask us not to reflect a value. A few items are extremely rare and we simply cannot apply a value. Some items are very scarce, with the value increasing rapidly, we left the high-side parameter open by stating "to market." One must always remember the actual value of an item is the price just negotiated between buyer and seller. Neither the Authors nor the Publisher assumes responsibility for any losses that might be incurred as a result of utilizing values reflected in this book.

American Glass Company
Carney, Kansas (affiliate of General Glassware)

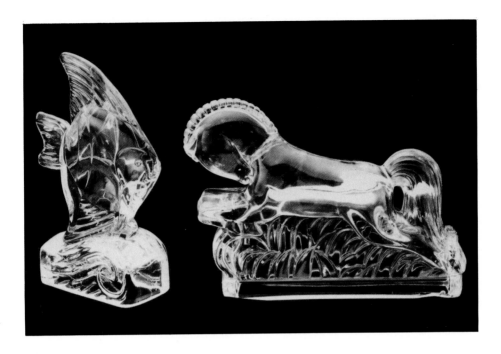

Angelfish Bookend. *Crystal, 8¼" high, solid glass. $60.00–70.00.*
Jumping Horse Bookend. *Crystal, 8" high., hollow base. (Also seen in frosted.)*
$45.00–55.00.

See Kenneth R. Haley bio, page 84.

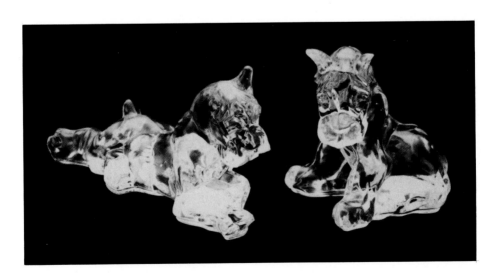

Boxer Dog. *Lying, 3⅞" high., crystal. $50.00–70.00.*
Boxer Dog. *Sitting, 4¾" high., crystal. $50.00–70.00.*
(Both dogs produced in frosted, with red nose and black eyes.)

NOTE: *Believed to be designed after the pair of dogs owned by Mr. Lowitz, president of American Glass Company.*

See Kenneth R. Haley bio, page 84.

Cambridge Glass Company
Cambridge, Ohio

Cambridge Advertising Sign. *This sign was given to stores marketing Cambridge glassware, to place in their display windows, show cases, or elsewhere in the store to let customers know that they had Cambridge for sale. This is one of several types of advertising signs made by Cambridge. This one is a combination of crystal and crystal satin glass.*

Cambridge Swan. *10". All information regarding Cambridge swans is contained in an article by Clyde E. Ingersoll found later in this chapter.*

The Cambridge Glass Company was founded in Cambridge, Ohio, and started producing glassware in 1902. Cambridge produced excellent quality handmade glass in crystal and many beautiful colors. Cambridge, like competitive companies of this era, applied various decorations, etchings, cuttings, and frosted some glass. Their frosting was referred to as satin. Cambridge, in addition to producing a general line of glassware, produced numerous novelty items, figural flower holders (referred to as frogs), animals, and many swans in several styles and multiple colors. Cambridge had a brief closing at the end of 1954, but was reopened and operated until 1958 when they had a final closing. Imperial Glass Company, Bellaire, Ohio, bought Cambridge assets which included a number of molds. Over the years Imperial used some of these molds to produce items in both crystal and Imperial colors. Imperial did alter some of the molds which enables one to tell the difference between an Imperial reissue and the original Cambridge production. Cambridge marked some of their glass with a triangle enclosing the letter "c." Much of their glassware came with a paper label. In 1985, the Cambridge molds in the Imperial factory at its closing were sold to several glass companies, perhaps some to individuals and some to National Cambridge Collectors, Inc.

Lion Bookend. *The Lion bookend was produced by Cambridge in crystal only. This figurine is 6" high and 5" long at the base. The Lion is solid glass; however, the base is hollow. Detail is good. The Lion appears to be standing with its front legs on a mound of dirt. His head is turned to the left with his mouth open as if "roaring." $100.00–125.00.*

Reissues: Imperial Glass Company, 1978, in amber, as a commemorative item for the National Cambridge Collectors, Inc. Marked "N.C.C." 1978 L.I.G. See page 41.

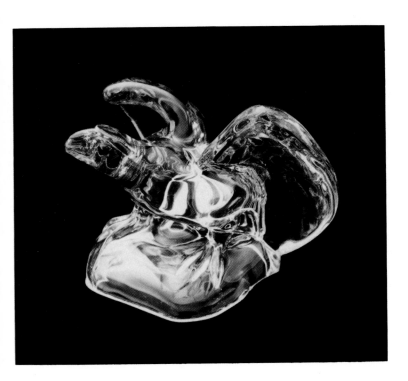

Eagle Bookend. *Cambridge produced the Eagle bookend in crystal, crystal satin, and crystal crown tuscan combination. This bookend is 5½" high (wing tip to bottom of base), 4" long, and 4" wide (base). Although the base and lower part of the figurine are hollow, most of the eagle is solid glass. Detail is good. His wings are up-lifted and the head is turned to the right. $60.00–80.00.*

Reissues: (Reportedly) Imperial Glass Company, in crystal 1964–1968. Mosser Glass Company, 1968, in cobalt for N.C.C. See page 41.

Eagle Bookend. *This Eagle bookend is a combination of crystal and crown tuscan. It is extremely rare.*
A suggested value cannot be placed on this item due to its extreme rarity.

Ladyleg Bookend. *The Ladyleg bookend was produced by Cambridge in crystal and crystal satin. They are 8" high. This item is solid glass and has good detail. $150.00-175.00 each.*

Reissues: Mosser Glass Company, 1977, in medium blue for the National Cambridge Collectors Inc., as a commemorative item. Also reissued in green carnival and custard. See page 228.

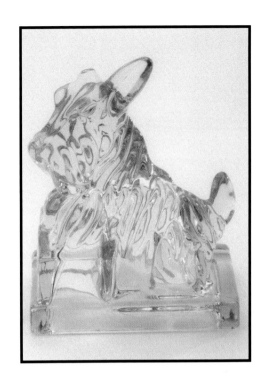

Scottie Bookend. The Scottie bookend was produced in crystal, crystal satin, milk glass, and ebony. The figurine is 6½" high (including base) and 5" long at the base. The bookend is a Scottie dog who has his front feet on what appears to be a box. His head is turned slightly to the left. His right ear is layed back and the left ear stands erect. The bookend, including the Scottie is hollow. $75.00–100.00.

Reissues: Imperial Glass Company, 1979, in black satin as a commemorative item for the National Cambridge Collectors, Inc. It is marked "N.C.C. 1979 L.I.G." Also made in caramel slag, marked ALIG. See page 41.

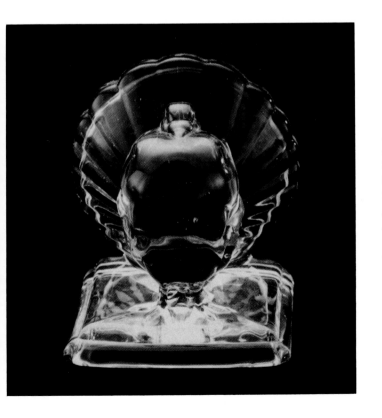

Pouter Pigeon Bookend. Cambridge produced the Pouter Pigeon bookend in crystal, milk glass, and crown tuscan. The bookend stands 5½" high (including the base) and is 3¼" by 5" at the base. The pigeon is solid glass and the base is hollow. Detail is good. The tail is fanned out forming almost a complete circle and the head is straight forward lying on the puffed-out breast. $50.00–70.00.

Reissues: None.

NOVELTY FIGURES

No. 1 Bird   No. 2 Bird   No. 3 Bird   Squirrel

Frog   1371 Bridge Hound   No. 1 Butterfly   No. 2 Butterfly   No. 3 Butterfly

The Cambridge Novelty figurines pictured above were made from approximately the mid 1930's until the mid 1950's. Most of the figurines have been reissued by other companies or molds made very similar to the original Cambridge molds. Some of the reissues are marked with the company logo, such as a capital "B" and a capital "M."

Birds: Cambridge made the birds in three styles as pictured above. They were made in crystal, crystal satin, light emerald, light emerald satin, and probably other colors. Has been reissued or a mold made very close to the original mold.

Squirrel: The squirrel was made in crystal, crystal satin, amber, amber satin, and probably in other colors. It has been reissued and bears the mark as stated above.

Frog: The frog was produced in crystal, crystal satin, light emerald, light emerald satin, and probably other colors. It has been reissued and in all probability bear the logo of the manufacturer.

Bridge Hound: Cambridge produced the bridge hound in multiple colors, including ebony, mocha, pistachio, gold krystol, dark amber, crown tuscan, milk, amethyst, blue, dark emerald, dianthus (peachblo), and perhaps others. They have a hole through their head which holds a pencil. They have been reissued in many colors and probably bear the mark of their producer.

Butterfly: The butterfly was produced by Cambridge in three styles as pictured above. They were sometimes referred to as "moths." They were made in crystal, crystal satin, dianthus (peachblo) both clear and satin, and probably other colors. They have been reissued.

No. 3 Bird. *2¾" long, crystal satin. $25.00–30.00.*
No. 2 Butterfly. *Reissue by Boyd.*
Frog. *1¾" high, dark emerald. $35.00–45.00.*
Frog. *Crystal satin. $20.00–25.00.*

Bridge Hound. *Left to right: 1¾" high. Amber, $25.00–30.00; ebony, $30.00–35.00; dark emerald, $25.00–30.00; dianthus (peachblo), $25.00–30.00.*

Cambridge produced two sizes of Rabbit covered boxes, 5" and 7". They were also produced at two different time periods. The older style has much more detail than the later productions. Obviously they reworked the molds and took out the fine detail. They were made in crystal, dianthus (peachblo), and perhaps other colors.

Cambridge Rabbit Covered Box. *7" new style, crystal. $150.00–175.00.*

Cambridge Rabbit Covered Box. *5" old style, dianthus (peachblo). $275.00–325.00.*

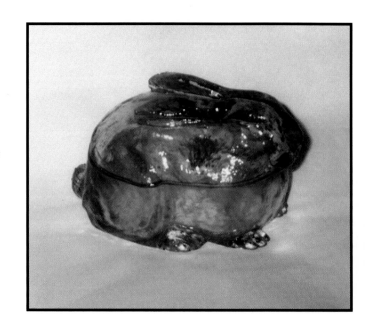

Cambridge Amber Turkey. $400.00–475.00.

Cambridge produced the Covered Turkey container for a period of ten years from approximately 1940 until 1950. They were made in multiple colors including amber, carmen, gold krystol, royal blue, dianthus (peachblo), Willow blue, emerald and, of course, crystal. The top of the tail is 7¼" high, while the base is 4¾" wide and 5¾" long. The tail feathers have a simple line down the middle of each feather and no other detail. Both feet are visible, with the right foot further extended than the left and he appears to be standing on a leaf-covered mound of dirt. Cambridge turkeys are often confused with turkeys made by L.E. Smith Company, by turkeys made for L.G. Wright, and turkeys made presumably by U.S. Glass. Cambridge is much larger than the Smith turkey, almost twice the size. See page 180 for comparison. Turkeys made for L.G. Wright have comparable detail; however, they were made in white milk glass, amethyst carnival, carnival with milk glass head, and milk glass body with a carnival head. The turkey presumably made by U.S. Glass causes the most confusion. See the following photo to see the many differences.

Non-Cambridge Turkey. Amber. $200.00–250.00.

The turkey pictured here **is not** Cambridge; however, it is most often confused with the Cambridge production. An 1898 U.S. Glass Company catalog shows a picture or drawing of this turkey container. There also has been speculation that this mold was an import. Nonetheless, there are several differences between the two even though they are comparable in size. The first major difference is the base. This turkey stands on a base which has a waffle appearance. The design would remind one of the old pattern glass cut block. The second major difference is the fine feather detail in the tail. The feathers are plain on the Cambridge production whereas the detail is so fine on this turkey that they appear much more like feathers. The popularity of the Cambridge turkeys have brought the price up on these turkeys, or perhaps it is because of the confusion.

Cambridge Glass Company produced swans from 1928 until closing in 1958. They were made in many colors, various sizes, and in different styles. Mr. Clyde E. Ingersoll, a leading authority on swans, graciously pre-

pared a very indepth article on Cambridge swans and gave permission for reprint in this book in order for us to share it with collectors.

Evolution of The Cambridge Swan Molds
by Clyde E. Ingersoll

This article is the result of examination of Cambridge swans and swans made in Cambridge molds by Mosser, Boyd, Levay (made by Imperial), Cambridge by Imperial, and Summit Art swans in my collection and at the NCC Museum. I am especially indebted to Bill Smith of NCC for giving me some exact dates of mold changes. My original premise was that all the molds were changed at the same time. After finding that that was not the case, some restudying of my collection brought about some changes in my conclusions and quite a change in this article.

We speak of Type I, Type II, and Type III swans; I don't know if anyone has defined what is meant by the three Types. I hope this article will give a definition, but it may not coincide with present conceptions. I will state the definition, as I see it, after I have given the EVOLUTION as I see it with the facts I have available.

The sizes of swans made by Cambridge starting in December 1928 were 3", 4½", 6½", 8½", 10", and 13", measured from tail to breast. I do not follow this way of measuring in my collection. I measure the overall length in centimeters. In either case, the size obtained is taken as a nominal value because the swans varied both in body length and overall length according to the amount of distortion, or shaping, that was produced while the glass was still hot. There is, of course, more variation in size when the overall measurement is taken because of the amount of head/neck adjustment while the glass was still pliable.

Cambridge introduced the swans identified by mold number only. In subsequent catalogs, they were identified by their various uses, as well as mold numbers.

3"	1040*	individual mint or nut: ashtray
4½"	1041*	candy dish
6½"	1042*	mayonnaise or candy dish
8½"	1043*	celery holder or bon-bon
10"	1044*	table decoration
13"	1045*	table centerpiece
4½"	1050*	candleholder; mold part ordered 4-4-52, but 1928 catalog page shows candleholder
10"	1052*	flower pot (apparently with an insert)
16"	1221	punch bowl, cup (introduced 1937)

8½"	1492	w/cover, candy box or bon-bon, (introduced 1-6-37) (thanks to Carl Beynon, Crystal Ball, Apr. 1989). Cover mold was junked in early 1940's; WW II scrap drive

The introductory design was the swan mold currently called Type I.

Figure 1. 3" Type I swan. All sizes were essentially the same.

Fall 1928, p.52: introduction, starred in above list

Type I – 3": 1928–1933
Type II – others: 1928–1939

All sizes of the Type I swan were the same design, but execution was slightly different. Some of the larger sizes have a lack of symmetry; the 8½" swan has 11 large wing feathers on one side and nine on the other. The 6½" swan has 10 and nine, the 4½" has 11 and 10. Only the 3" swan has 10 on each side. The obvious feature of all Type I molds is the feather detail, not only on the large feathers, but on smaller wing, breast, and tail feathers.

Figure 2. Feather detail of Type I, 8½" swan.

In the catalog reprint from the National Cambridge Collectors, we find the following:

Jan. 1930, p48:	Type I swans in sizes 3"–13"
Early 1931, p17-31:	8½" swan, Type I
Early 1933, p30-33:	8½" swan, Type I 3" swan, #1040 1/2; Type II
1937, pages from Crystal Ball, Oct '85:	3" swan, Type II; designated #1040 (in error? Type II is 1040 1/2); 4½" to 13" swans; Type I.
1-23-39, mold order books from Bill Smith	'Change all swans to be like #1043 (8½") sample' (details removed)

We can conclude from these entries that the change from Type I to Type II for the 3" swan occurred in 1933. The mold order book entry indicates that the change from the original, for other sizes, took place in 1939. It may be assumed that the original 3" mold was also changed in 1939, even though it had not been used since 1933.

Type II – 3": 1933–1939 (#1040 1/2)

The reworked Type I 3" mold (#1040) was apparently never used by Cambridge, but was sold to Imperial with the other Cambridge molds. When Imperial went out of business, this mold was purchased by Boyd's Crystal Art Glass and used to make many colors not made by Cambridge.

The 3" Type II (1040 1/2) was a new mold, with somewhat different design. It had the C in a triangle. It featured somewhat spread wingtips and the large wing feathers were more "swept back." A deep notch separated the tail from the wings. A feature of the 3" Type II was a "dimple" in the wings and the area around the dimple was a "mottled" effect, without the "blister" effect found on other sizes. The 3" Type II swan was a little longer,

measured tail to breast, but it was still called a 3" swan and the mold number was 1040 1/2 (although later the 1040 number appears again, possibly by mistake: the 1949 catalog carries a reprint page from the 1940 catalog).

Figure 3. 3" Type II – #1040 1/2.

Some of the differences between Type I (#1040) and Type II (#1040 1/2) can be readily seen:

Type I   no notch; flat tail surface; upright wing feathers

Type II   notch between tail and wings; fan-like tail; swept back wing feathers

Other features of the Type II take a closer look: The detail of the major wing feathers consist mostly of a central spine for each feather; the balance of the wing is an indistinct pattern; simply "lumpy"; the wing includes a "dimple."

Type II – other sizes: 1939–1940

Figure 4. Feather detail of Type II 6½": smooth feathers of the reworked mold.

The other sizes were reworked in 1939 (rework order of 23 Jan. 1939.) The reworking consisted of: Removing feather detail, which left the large feathers with only outline and smooth rounded surface within the outline; the under-tail feathers became "blister" shaped; most of the neck was made smooth; and the mold mark, C in a triangle, was removed by polishing it away. In the 4½" and 6½" molds, however, the polishing away was incomplete, so the C and the triangle can still be discerned on some swans made in these molds. Milk glass swans that I have in the 4½" and 6½" sizes do not have any vestige of the mark, and 6½" swans made by Imperial do not have any vestige, so it must have been completely removed at a later date.

Comparing Figure 4 with Figure 1, the difference is obvious; all feathers have lost their detail. I have not seen any pictures or catalog pages from the Jan.1939–Feb. 1940 period. Bill says that there was no Type II in the larger swans. This is a question of definition of the Types. Bill says they went from Type I to Type III in the larger than 3" molds. If we define Types simply by change in the product, the 1939 change would have resulted in a Type II. It is hard to believe that no swans were made in the newly reworked molds, so we assume that there were some Type II swans of the larger sizes made for a short time; after Jan. 1939 to sometime after the plugs to flare the wings were made after Feb. 1940. These were the same shape as those made presently by Boyd and Summit. Imperial also made some in this configuration for Levay. I have three swans, 8½", that might be identified as Type II, two crown tuscan and one carmen. There appears to be no flare.

In the catalog reprints from NCC and mold order books, we find the following:

Feb.1940	Mold order books; "Make plugs to flare the wings on all size swans."
June 1949 p19	1221 Punch bowl (drawing, not a picture) seems to be Type II (no flare)
June 1949 p21	Catalog page of "Smokers' Items" shows a 3" (1040) still in Type II. Bill tells me that this page is a reprint of a 1940 catalog, so this would be misleading in dating the change.
June 1949 p23,31	Other catalog pages of the same date shows five sizes, all Type III and the page titled "Swans." The 3" can be identified as Type III because of the "blister" effect feathers on the wing. Again the 1040 designation is used for the 3" mold.
Aug. 1949 p152, 152-B	3", 6½", 8½" shown in Type III. 3" again identified as 1040.

From these entries, we can conclude that the change from Type II to Type III took place in 1939 for the 3" swan, the Type III apparently reverted to the #1040 mold designation.

The change from Type II to Type III in larger sizes took place in 1940 after the flaring tools were made.

Type III 3": 1939–1958

The 3" mold, 1040 1/2, Type II was reworked, and returned to the 1040 mold designation. It is not this simple, however. The change took place in two steps: IIIA was produced in the reworked Type II mold (1939–1940) and Type IIIB was produced in the same mold with the flaring tool (1940–1958).

Figure 5. Type IIIA was made in the reworked Type II mold.

- The wing feathers were almost verticle.
- Swan was a little longer from tail to breast.
- It had the "blister" shaped feather structure on the breast and under the tail.
- The "dimple" in the wing was removed, forming the "blister" shaped feather detail on the wings where the "dimple" had been.
- The neck was smoothed.
- The large wing feather detail was removed so the feathers were like the larger size swans.
- The tail was made more round instead of squared off as in Type II.
- The C in a triangle mark was removed.

Figure 6. 3" Type IIIB. Same mold as IIIA but with the spreader.

Type IIIB had a further spreading of the wings and wider internal dimension due to the use of the new plug, so that the cavity was closer to round instead of oval as in Types I and II.

Figure 6 shows the change made from the Type IIIA: The wings are spread to a sharp angle.

The distinction between Type IIIA and IIIB is not as obvious as one might think. When a group of Type III swans is put on a table together, Type IIIA can be distinguished from Type IIIB by the width across the wings, or when looking from the rear, the angle of the wings can be seen, but when observed one at a time, as when buying, it is not so easy. Particularly, if you find an unmarked Mosser swan. The Mosser swans are made in the Type III mold without the spreader and are therefore the same as Type IIIA swans. The key to the distinction is mold wear. During many years of usage certain defects appeared in the mold; a small projection on the swan's left foot and the left foot became

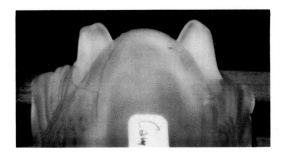

Figure 7. 3" Type IIIB swan bottom view showing feet.

broader; the difference in width of the left and right feet is quite obvious. Less obvious is a mold closure defect in front of the swan's right wing (on marked Mosser).

Figure 7 shows a Type IIIB swan from the bottom so the feet can be seen. The two feet are essentially the same and the same as the feet on the Type II and the Type IIIA. This means that the change in the left foot did not take place until after 1940 when the spreader was first used.

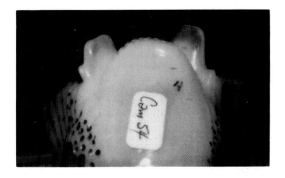

Figure 8. 3" Type IIIB swan bottom view showing projection from left foot.

Figure 8 shows the start of the left foot change. A projection has started to "grow" near where the foot joins the body. We don't have any way of dating the start of growth of this projection; only that it was after 1940 and before 1954.

Figure 9. 3" Type IIIB swan, bottom view showing the broadening of the left foot.

Figure 9 shows how the mold makers handled the projection; they smoothed it out, making the foot broader than the original. Again, we have no way of dating the mold adjustment. We can give a limit; however, milk glass was made only in 1954, and the 3" Type IIIB milk glass swan had the broad left foot, so it was before 1954.

Figure 10. Mosser swan made in the Type IIIA configuration mold. Bottom view.

Figure 11. Comparison of swans made with and without the flaring tool – both by Imperial.

Figure 10 shows the added projection on the left foot of a Mosser swan. It is not known whether Cambridge made swans in the mold when it got into this condition. The milk glass swan in my collection, however, has the beginning of this added projection. It is not visible to photograph, but it can be felt.

A less obvious difference between unmarked Mosser swans and Cambridge Type IIIA swans is a mold closure defect in front of the swan's right wing (on marked Mosser swans, this defect seems to have been fixed). The defect is a small amount of glass that is extruded between mold parts (a small flash). This defect is not present on the milk glass swan, but there seems to be a beginning of it on the Type II swan, so it may be related to the use of the mold without the spreader.

This mold, with its defects due to long use, without the "spreader plug" is the one obtained by Mosser. It has been said that the elder Mosser obtained it when he left Cambridge Glass. It has been used by Mosser for many colors similar to ones used by Cambridge as well as many other colors. Mosser made swans with this mold without the flaring tool since 1960 without any marking. In the early 1980's, a mold mark was added; M in an Ohio outline.

Type III other sizes: 1940–1958

For the other sizes, the change from Type II to Type III consisted of a manipulation after the swan was removed from the mold; while the glass was still pliable, a flaring tool was forced into the back of the swan to bend the wing "feathers" outwardly.

Imperial used the flaring tool for swans they made and paper-labelled "Cambridge by Imperial." They did not use the flaring tool for swans they made for distribution by Levay. There was no mark on the Levay 6½" swans, so they may be confused with Cambridge Type II.

When Summit Art Glass borrowed the 8½" mold from Imperial, they didn't get, or didn't use, the flaring tool. These swans may be confused with Cambridge Type II swans since Summit didn't mark them.

According to NCC's reproduction of the Cambridge catalog of 1949 through 1953, (the NCC Color book indicates that milk glass was produced only from Feb. 1954 to the plant closing in July 1954) swans in milk glass had different mold numbers:

3"	W94	4½" candle	W98
4½"	W95	16" punch cup	W99
6½"	W96	punch cup	W100
8½"	W97		

Although the mold numbers are different, the swans that I have seen are from the same molds.

Definition: There are two possible definitions of the Types:

1. Whenever the product changed, a new Type was formed. The result of this definition would be:

Four types for 3":
I – Original #1040
II – New mold #1040 1/2
III – Reworked #1040 1/2 (#1040) mold
IV – Reworked mold with flaring tool

Three types for larger sizes:
I – Original
II – Reworked mold
III – Reworked mold with flaring tool

2. Types were defined by new or reworked mold:

Two types for larger swans:
I – Original
II – Reworked mold (with or without the flaring tool)

Three types for 3":
I – Original #1040
II – New mold #1040 1/2
III – Reworked #1040 1/2 (#1040) mold (with or
without the flaring tool)

I tend to favor a combination of these definitions as more in keeping with what I believe is the common perception.

3" swan:
Type I – Original mold; good feather detail
Type II – New mold
Type IIIA – Reworked Type II mold
Type IIIB – IIIA with flaring tool

All larger sizes:
Type I – Original mold
Type II – Reworked original mold
Type III – Type II with flaring tool

Summary:

3" swan:
Dec. 1928: Type I – #1040 introduced
1933: Type II – #1040 1/2 introduced
1939: Type I – #1040 mold modified but not used
1939: Type IIIA – #1040 developed from Type II – #1040 1/2
1940: Type IIIB – #1040; flaring tool used with modified Type II mold
1958: Type I – #1040 sold to Imperial
1958: Type IIIA – #1040 obtained by Mosser. First swans made were unmarked: later marked with M in Ohio outline

1985: Type I as modified, sold to Boyd's Crystal Art Glass at closing of Imperial. All swans made in this mold by Boyd were marked with Boyd's B in a diamond.

4½" swan – #1041
6½" swan – #1042
8½" swan – #1043
10" swan – #1044
13" swan – #1045

Dec. 1928: Type I – #1041–#1045 introduced
1939: Type II – #1041–#1045; feather detail removed from Type I mold
1940: Type III – #1041–#1045; flaring tool made; mold unchanged
1949: Type III 13" – #1045; no longer in catalog; mold may have gone into WW II scrap drive
1958: Type III – #1041–#1045 sold to Imperial
1958-85: Some 6½" – #1042 (Type II) made for Levay
Some 6½" – #1042, 8½" – #1043 and 10" – #1044 (Type III) labelled as "Cambridge by Imperial" were made and sold by Imperial
1985: Type III 4½" – #1041 sold to Boyd's Crystal Art Glass at closing of Imperial. All swans made in this mold by Boyd were marked with Boyd's B in a diamond.

Type III 6½" – #1042, 8½" – #1043 and 10" – #1044 sold to Summit Art Glass at closing of Imperial. First swans made with only a projection "pimple" in center of bottom. Also, Summit borrowed the #1043 mold from Imperial for a trial period before Imperial's demise and these were made with no marking at all.

Measurements reflected for the following swans are given in the sizes that Cambridge advertised as production sizes although there are slight variations which are commonly found in handmade glass. Swans are pictured by color rather than style.

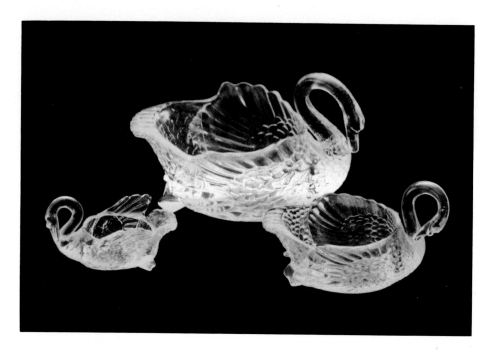

Cambridge Swans. *Left to right: Crystal. 3", $20.00–25.00. 6½", $30.00–35.00. 4½", $25.00–30.00.*

Cambridge Swans. *Left to right: 3" crown tuscan, $40.00–50.00. 6½" milk glass, $125.00–150.00. 4½" milk glass, $75.00–100.00.*

Cambridge Swans. *Left to right: Light emerald. 10", $100.00–125.00. 3", $35.00–45.00. 4½", $45.00–55.00.*

Cambridge Swans. *Left to right: Dianthus (peachblo). 8½", $70.00–80.00. 3", $35.00–45.00.*

Cambridge Swans. *Left to right: Carmen. 8½", $225.00–275.00. 6½", $175.00–225.00.*

Cambridge Swan. *Ebony. 8½", $125.00–150.00.*

Swan Punch Bowl Set. *Crystal. Punch bowl, 16" long, $500.00–600.00. Punch cup, 3½" high, $45.00–65.00. Base, $75.00–100.00.*

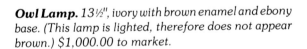

Owl Lamp. *13½", ivory with brown enamel and ebony base. (This lamp is lighted, therefore does not appear brown.) $1,000.00 to market.*

Cambridge Glass Company made a number of figural flower holders from the mid 1920's until the factory closed in 1958. These flower holders are commonly referred to as "frogs." Many of the molds were scrapped by Cambridge as part of the war effort in the 1940's; however, some of the molds survived and went to Imperial Glass Company, where some of the frogs were reissued. Imperial changed the base and instead of being smooth they put vertical ribs on the base. After Imperial closed, the flower frog molds were sold, but the bases still have the vertical ribs. The following photos reflect the various flower holders made, as well as the sizes and many colors. Leading the parade are the Elegant Ladies that are so popular among collectors today.

Rose Lady. *8½", low base, amber satin, siting in a floral /candleholder centerpiece. (See Rose Lady later in this chapter for colors, sizes, and prices.)*

Mandolin Lady. *9½", crystal satin, sitting in a floral / candleholder centerpiece. (See Mandolin Lady later in this chapter for colors, sizes, and prices.)*

The Draped Lady figural flower holder is seen more often than any of the other Cambridge figural flower holders, except for perhaps the Seagull. She came in three sizes, 8½", 12¾", and 13¼". The latter has a vertical fluted base; in other words, it is not perfectly round. The 8½" figurine was reissued by Imperial Glass Company during 1962 in crystal with a lalique finish. The Imperial reissues have vertical ribs around the base. They have also been reissued by other companies since Imperial closed, in light blue, cobalt, and ruby. They also have the vertical ribs around the base.

Draped Lady. *8½" high, dianthus (peachblo). $100.00–125.00.*

Draped Lady. *Left to right: 8½" high, satin finish. Light emerald, $100.00–125.00. Amber, $175.00–200.00. Dianthus, (peachblo), $100.00–125.00. Gold krystol, $200.00–250.00.*

Draped Lady. *Left to right: 8½". Crystal, $50.00–75.00. Amber, $150.00–175.00. Ivory, $750.00 to market. Light emerald, $75.00–100.00. Crystal, $50.00–75.00.*

Draped Lady. *Left to right: 8½". Gold krystol, $200.00–250.00. Dianthus (peachblo), $100.00–125.00. Crown tuscan, rarity prohibits pricing. Moonlight blue, $325.00–375.00. Amber, $150.00–175.00.*

Draped Lady. *Left to right: 12¾", satin. Light emerald, $200.00–225.00. Crystal, $150.00–175.00. Amber, $250.00–275.00.*

Draped Lady. *Left to right: 13¼", high base (fluted). Amber, $250.00–275.00. Bluebell, $550.00–650.00. Ivory, $925.00 to market. Light emerald, $225.00–250.00. Crystal, $175.00–200.00.*

Bashful Charlotte was produced by Cambridge in two sizes, 6½" and 11½". This elegant flower holder is a lady who is partially covered with a towel or cloth and appears to be struggling to cover herself. She is bent forward with her right hand holding the cloth over her breast and her left arm and hand extend downward towards her right knee. Both sizes have been reissued. Imperial Glass Company has been given credit for altering the mold and adding vertical ribs to the bases, hollowing out the base, and removing the holes in the 6½" figurine. Imperial referred to this flower holder as "Venus Rising" when producing for Mirror Images. The 6½" Bashful Charlotte has been reissued in multiple colors and the 11½" in cobalt and possibly vaseline. Imperial reissued the 6½" in seven different colors. These have IG-81 in the base. See page 124.

The next three photos reflect Bashful Charlotte in crystal and several of the colors produced by Cambridge.

Bashful Charlotte. *11½", moonlight blue.*
$500.00–550.00.

Bashful Charlotte. *Left to right: 6½". Moonlight blue, $400.00–450.00. Amber, $350.00–400.00. Crystal (side view), $75.00–100.00. Light emerald, $125.00–150.00. Crystal (front view), $75.00–100.00. Dianthus (peachblo), $125.00–150.00.*

Bashful Charlotte. *Left to right: 11½". Moonlight blue, $500.00–550.00. Dianthus (peachblo), $350.00–375.00. Crystal, $150.00–175.00. Moonlight blue satin, $550.00–600.00.*

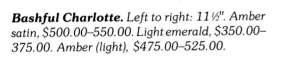

Bashful Charlotte. *Left to right: 11½". Amber satin, $500.00–550.00. Light emerald, $350.00–375.00. Amber (light), $475.00–525.00.*

Cambridge produced the Rose Lady in two sizes, the low base being 8½" high and the high base 9¾" high. Both sizes were produced in multiple colors. The figurine is a lady holding a bouquet of flowers, presumably roses. Her right hand is chest high above the flowers and her left arm and hand are waist high cradling the flowers. Her head is down as if she is admiring her flowers. The Rose Lady has not been reissued.

Rose Lady. *8½" high, light emerald.*
$175.00–200.00.

Rose Lady. *Left to right: 8½" high. Amber, $175.00–200.00. Light emerald satin, $200.00–225.00. Dianthus (peachblo) $175.00–200.00. Light emerald, $175.00–200.00. Dianthus (peachblo) satin, $200.00–225.00. Crystal satin, $150.00–175.00.*

Rose Lady. *Left to right: 9¾" high base. Amber satin, $275.00–300.00. Dianthus (peachblo), $250.00–275.00. Ivory, $850.00 to market. Amber, $250.00–275.00. Crystal, $175.00–200.00. Light emerald, $250.00–275.00.*

Draped Lady and Rose Lady. *Left to right: Very scarce opaques. Draped Lady, 8½", ivory. $750.00 to market. Draped Lady, 8½", crown tuscan, rarity prohibits pricing. Draped Lady, 13¼", ivory, $925.00 to market. Rose Lady, 9¾", ivory, $850.00 to market.*

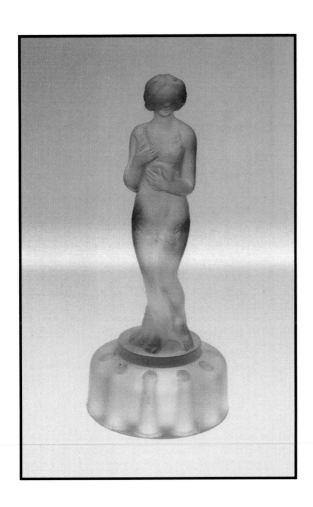

Cambridge produced the Mandolin Lady in one size only,
9½" high. This figurine was produced in crystal, light
emerald, and dianthus (peachblo). Each was also available
in satin. This flower holder is a lady playing a mandolin.
Her right hand is holding the neck of the instrument while
she is playing it with her left hand. The Mandolin Lady has
not been reissued.

Mandolin Lady. *9½" high, dianthus (peachblo)
satin. $375.00–425.00.*

Mandolin Lady. *Left to right: Crystal (side view, bent), $200.00–250.00. Dianthus (peachblo) satin,
$375.00–425.00. Crystal (head forward), $200.00–250.00. Dianthus (peachblo), $350.00–400.00.
Crystal (head turned), $200.00–250.00. Light emerald, $350.00–400.00.*

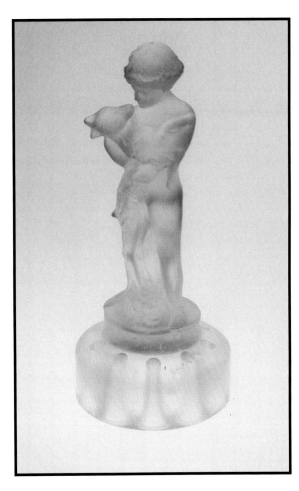

Cambridge produced theTwo-Kid flower holder in only one size, 9¼" high. Some were produced with an oval base but they were the same height. This figurine was produced in multiple colors. The Two-Kid flower holder is a youngster cradling a small animal (presumably a baby goat based on terminology) in its arms. The Two-Kid was not reissued.

Two-Kid. *9¼" high, light emerald satin. $325.00–350.00.*

Two-Kid. *Left to right: 9¼" high. Amber satin, $350.00–400.00. Dianthus (peachblo), $250.00–275.00. Crystal, $175.00–200.00. Amber, $300.00–325.00. Light emerald, $250.00–275.00. Dianthus (peachblo), $250.00–275.00.*

Cambridge produced two types of Geisha flower holders, one-bun and two-bun. They were produced in multiple colors, including opaques of jade, ivory, and perhaps others. All one has to do is look at their hairstyle to determine if they are a one-bun or a two-bun. The bottom of the figurine is threaded and screws into the base. This figurine was not reissued.

Geishas. *One-bun, amber, $500.00–600.00. Two-bun, crystal, $300.00–400.00. One-bun, crystal, $300.00–400.00.*

Cambridge produced the Melon Boy, sometimes referred to as Boy Child, in only one size, 9¾" high. They were produced in only two colors, dianthus (peachblo) and light emerald. Both colors came in satin. The figurine is that of a young boy holding what appears to be half of a melon. The Melon Boy was not reissued.

Melon Boy. *Dianthus (peachblo), $400.00–500.00. Light emerald, $500.00–550.00.*

Draped Lady. *Left to right: Dianthus (peachblo), 8½", $275.00–300.00. Light emerald, 8½", $275.00–300.00. Crystal, 8½", $175.00–200.00. Crystal satin, 8½", $200.00–225.00.*
Two-Kid. *Dianthus (peachblo), 9", $350.00–375.00. Light emerald, 9", $300.00–325.00.*
Draped Lady. *Dianthus (peachblo), 8½", $275.00–300.00.*

Cambridge produced the Eagle flower holder in the late 1920's. An official name was not found in Cambridge records, so it was named Eagle by collectors. It was produced in amber, dianthus (peachblo), emerald, and crystal, and is 5⅝" tall. It has not been reissued.

Eagle. *Dianthus (peachblo). $450.00 to market.*

Although Cambridge records have not been found that will support this flower holder being produced by Cambridge, the color is right and the dimensions of the base are the same as the Eagle. We will simply refer to it as a Bird on a Stump. It is 5⅜" high and has only been seen in light emerald. Reissues have not been seen.

Bird on a Stump. *Light emerald, $350.00 to market.*

37

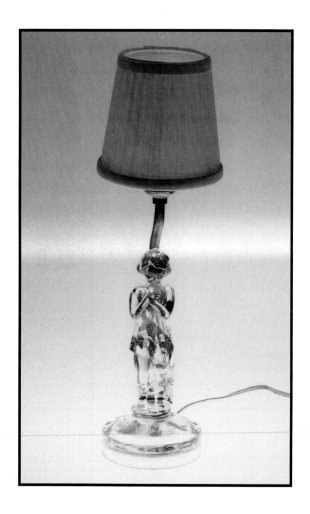

Cambridge made several of the figural flower frogs into figurines and figurals for lamps. The Geishas and Buddhas had screw bottoms which screwed into a base. The Two-Kid and Bashful Charlotte were smooth on the bottom and have been seen affixed to night light lamps. One would assume that the figurine was glued to the base. The Draped Lady lamp was a molded one-piece figurine and base. The base is hollow and has a hole in it for the cord. A brass tube was attached to the base behind the figurine and extended upwards and held the light socket and shade. Cambridge made these in crystal only. They have been reissued in green.

Draped Lady Lamp. *Crystal.*
$150.00–175.00.

Figurines or figurals for lamps.

Bashful Charlotte. *Crystal satin. $100.00–125.00.*
Draped Lady. *Light emerald satin. $125.00–150.00.*
Draped Lady. *Crystal satin. $100.00–125.00.*

Cambridge produced the Heron flower frogs in two sizes, 12" and 9". The 12" is the older of the two with production starting in the late 1920's. It was made only in crystal and was not reissued. Although there is reference to different 9" Herons, it obviously refers to the different number given to the milk glass Heron produced in the early 1950's. The molds were the same. The sides of the base are fluted on the 9" whereas the base is smooth on the 12". The 9" Heron, like the 12" Heron, has not been reissued. The small Heron is sometimes confused with the Heron produced by Duncan. See page 47 to see the difference.

Heron. *12", crystal. $85.00–125.00.*
Heron. *9", crystal. $50.00–75.00.*

The Blue Jay flower holder was produced in crystal, crystal satin, moonlight blue, emerald, Mandarin gold, and possibly other colors. The Blue Jay was also made without the base. It is 4½" high and has a peg bottom which fits a candle socket. The Blue Jay has not been reissued.

Blue Jay. *5½"high, on base, crystal. $125.00–150.00. Peg only, crystal, $125.00–150.00.*

The Sea Gull flower holder was produced in crystal and crystal satin. Production started in the late 1930's and probably continued until Cambridge closed. The Sea Gull is seen quite frequently. It was reissued by Imperial in the early 1960's. The reissue by Imperial reportedly has a ribbed base whereas the base on the Cambridge production was smooth.

Sea Gull. *Crystal. $50.00–75.00. Crystal satin (not shown), $55.00–80.00.*

Cambridge produced two types of turtle flower holders. The first (not pictured) was produced probably in the early 1920's and the second was produced circa 1940. Basically there is very little difference except in the top (the turtle's back). The early turtle was nearly flat whereas the later version is domed. Both had 19 holes and are 3½" wide and 5¼" long. They have been found in crystal, crystal satin, cobalt, ebony, green, and crown tuscan. They probably exist in other colors.

Turtles. *Crystal satin, $150.00–175.00. Ebony, $200.00–225.00.*

Cambridge produced Buddhas in two sizes in the late 1920's, 7¾" and 5½". Both came with flat bottoms or with a glass thread (resembles a large coin) on the bottom. This thread was used to attach the Buddha to a lamp base. The larger of the two came in crystal and several colors including light emerald, amber, and dianthus (peachblo). The small one came in crystal, amber, topaz, light emerald, dianthus (peachblo), bluebell, and perhaps other colors. They are solid glass and have excellent detail. Cambridge Buddhas are sometimes confused with those made by Gillinder & Sons, although when compared there are significant differences. See page 221 for comparison.

Buddha. *Amber, 5½", $200.00–250.00. Light emerald, 7¾", $300.00–350.00.*

The National Cambridge Collectors, Inc., had four items reissued out of original Cambridge molds as commemorative items. The first item (not pictured) was the Ladyleg bookend produced in 1977 by Mosser Glass Company. There were approximately 250 bookends made in medium blue and sold to the public for $32.50 each. See page 10 for description of the Ladyleg bookend.

Above Left: **1978 Commemorative Lion Bookend.** *Amber. This item was produced for N.C.C. by Lenox–Imperial Glass Company and was marked N.C.C. 1978 L.I.G. They sold to the public for $30.00 each.*

Above Right: **1979 Commemorative Scottie Dog Bookend.** *Black satin. This item was produced for N.C.C. by Lenox–Imperial Glass Company, and sold to the public for $30.00 each. They are marked N.C.C. 1979 L.I.G.*

Right: **1986 Commemorative Eagle Bookend.** *Cobalt. This item was produced for N.C.C. by Mosser Glass Company. The Eagle bookend sold to the public for $30.00.*

Co-Operative Flint Glass Company
Beaver Falls, Pennsylvania

**Frog and Cover. Pink, 4" high, 5½" long, circa 1927. Made in crystal and transparent colors. (Can be found in milk glass, manufactured by Vallerystahl in the 1920's.)

Note: Reissued by Erskine Glass Company in 1969 in amber and green.

Known originally as Beaver Falls Co-Operative Glass Company, this firm began operations in 1879, locating in Beaver Falls, Pennsylvania. With a name change in 1889, the company became Co-Operative Flint Glass Company.

This company was known for its extensive line of gift items, as well as soda fountain and restaurant ware. Losing the battle of the Depression Era, Co-Operative Flint closed its doors in 1934, leaving behind a wide range of colors and collectibles.

"Transparent" colors would include green, amber, ritz blue, rose, aqua blue, and ruby (black was also in the line). Ruby, and/or black animals command a 50% hike in value.

The two-piece bear, page 44 and the two-piece frog, have been found in milk glass, a Vallerystahl production of the early 1920's.

*Note: Items in this chapter preceded by double asterisk (**) are from a private collection and cannot be priced.

42

The two-piece elephant dish, while originating at the old Co-Operative Flint Glass Company works, was made at the Consolidated Lamp and Glass Company at Coraopolis, Pennsylvania and eventually at Erskine Glass Company, Wellsburg, West Virginia.

See Indiana Glass Company, page 145 for further production.

Controversy still exists with regard to Fenton's possible production of this mold.

**Elephant. *Two-piece dish, amber, 4½" high, 7" long, circa 1930. (Made in crystal and transparent colors and black.) This elephant was also made with variations of the back such as holes for flowers, and an ashtray with cigarette rests.*

Elephant. *Two-piece dish, plain back, ritz blue, 4½" high, 7" long, circa 1930. Rare color. $125.00–150.00.*

Elephant. *Two-piece with dish back, ruby, 4½" high, 7" long, circa 1930. Rare design and color. $150.00–175.00.*

Bear and Cover. *Amber, 1928. $300.00–350.00.*

Elephant. *Two-piece dish, bottom, amber, 4½" high x 7" long, 1927. Complete, $35.00–45.00.*

Both animals came in crystal and transparent colors. The bear has been found in milk glass. The bear mold was scrapped during WW II.

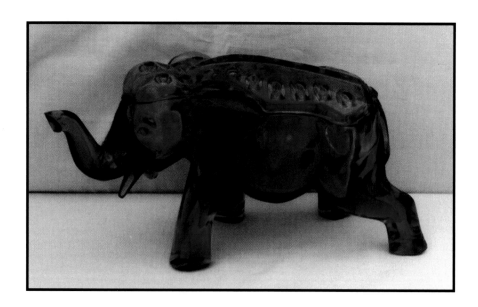

*****Large Elephant.*** *Flower block for back, green, 6" high x 13" long, circa 1927. (Also came with flat back.) Colors documented are crystal, black satin, and ruby.*

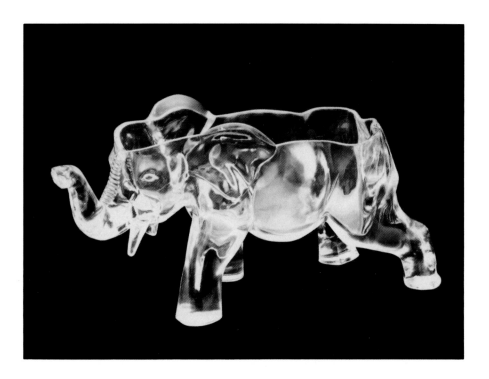

Large Elephant. *Missing back, crystal, 6" high x 13" long, circa 1927. Complete, $125.00–150.00.*

****Whale and Cover.** *Crystal, circa 1927. Made in crystal and transparent colors.*

Note: This mold was scrapped during World War II.

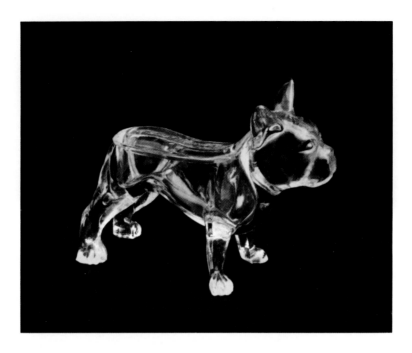

**#570 Dog and Cover. *Crystal, 5¼" long, circa 1927. Made in crystal and transparent colors, some hand decorated.*

**Cat and Cover. *Crystal, circa 1927. Made in crystal and transparent colors and black glass.*

Duncan Glass Company

Crystal Heron. This Heron is 7" tall and the ground and polished base is 2½" in diameter. The figurine is solid glass and has excellent detail. His right leg and foot are completely visible and extend to the ground. His left leg is drawn up underneath his body and only his left foot is visible. This figurine was produced in crystal and crystal satin. No reissues are known. $100.00–125.00.

Duncan Advertising Sign. This was distributed for use in windows and on shelves in stores selling Duncan glass.

Crystal Satin Heron. Details are the same as listed above for the Crystal Heron. $95.00–120.00.

Duncan glass has roots dating back to the mid 1800's, in the person of George Duncan. Although he had worked in various capacities for glass companies, it was not until 1874, that he actually had his own factory. He took over the Ripley and Company factory, Pittsburgh, Pennsylvania, in a partnership with his two sons and son-in-law. The company was known as George Duncan and Sons Company. His son-in-law, A.H. Heisey, later founded the Heisey Glass Company in Newark, Ohio. George Duncan died three years later in 1877. The company continued operations until the factory was destroyed by fire in 1892. The firm moved to Washington, Pennsylvania, where a new factory was built. The company was reorganized in 1900 and became known as the Duncan Miller Glass Company, although glassware continued to be marketed as "Genuine Duncan." The molds and equipment were sold to the U.S. Glass Company, in mid 1955. One year later the Duncan factory was destroyed by fire.

This is a mere capsulization of an extensive history on Duncan Glass, which has been written many times. During the productive life of this fine company, extensive lines of quality handmade glassware were produced. "Genuine Duncan" included pressed glass, blown, cuttings, etchings, crystal, and color. Duncan could "do it all."

This chapter encompasses only a few of the thousands of items produced by Duncan. Duncan, like competitive companies, produced glass animals, including lines of glass swans.

Crystal Dove, Head Down. *Crystal, $150.00–175.00.*

Dove on Bust-Off. *Crystal. The dove on the right is still on the bust-off just like it came out of the mold at the factory. Normally these were removed and the bottom was ground and polished. On bust-off, $150.00–175.00.*

Duncan produced the dove in crystal and crystal satin. From the tip of the tail to the tip of the beak it measures 11½". It is solid glass and has excellent detail. The bottom was ground on different angles, thus changing the height of the head. At least four different angles have been seen. The dove was originally sold with an oval solid glass base. It appears that only a few have survived. They have not been reissued.

Ruffed Grouse. *Rarity prohibits pricing.*

This Duncan grouse was made in crystal, crystal frosted, and crystal with frosted highlights on tail and collar. 1940's, it is 6½" high and 7½" long from tip of tail to breast. This figurine is solid glass and has excellent detail. This guy is extremely rare. Because of its design with tail extended, obviously many were broken. This, coupled with the fact that only a small number were made, accounts for its extreme rarity. It has not been reissued.

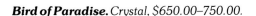

This Duncan product is from the 1930's. It is 8½" high and 13" long from tip of tail to tip of beak. This figurine is solid glass and has excellent detail. This elegant animal is sometimes referred to as a "peacock." Although the Bird of Paradise is rare, it is seen more often than the Ruffed Grouse. It has not been reissued.

Bird of Paradise. *Crystal, $650.00–750.00.*

Donkey, Cart, and Peon. *Three-piece set, crystal. $450.00–550.00.*

Note: There is a donkey look-alike made by Kanawha Glass Company, Dunbar, West Virginia. This donkey is almost identical to the donkey made by Duncan. The Kanawha donkey does not have the straps for the harness and ears are together and even whereas the Duncan donkey's ears are tipped with the left ear being lower. The Kanawha donkey is 4" long and 3½" high, while the Duncan donkey is 4¾" high and 4¾" long.

The Donkey, Cart, and Peon were made in crystal, crystal satin, and crystal with frosted highlights. All three pieces were solid glass except for the inside of the box on the cart and all have excellent detail. It is difficult to find the set and even more difficult to find the set not damaged.

The Donkey is 4¾" high from top of right ear to bottom of front feet. It is 4¾" long from front to back feet. He has a strap representing harness across his back and along both sides. His ears are tilted forward together, with the left being slightly lower than the right.

The two wheel cart is 3½" wide from wheel to wheel, 5½" long (overall length) and 3" high. The shafts of the cart, which go on each side of the donkey, are very vulnerable and easily broken.

The Peon is 5½" high. His head and face are not

visible. It has the appearance of a hat setting on a pair of shoulders.

Reissues: Fenton Glass Company bought the molds for the Donkey and Cart from U.S. Glass Company in 1964 and reissued them as follows: Donkey reissued in white satin, blue satin, crystal satin, custard (with daisies), French opalescent, and burmese. The Cart was reissued in white satin, blue satin, crystal satin, and burmese.

Fenton Glass Company made Commemorative Donkey and Cart for the Duncan Glass Society, Inc., as follows: 1986 – blue opalescent Donkey; 1987 – blue opalescent Cart; 1988 – topaz opalescent Donkey; 1989 – topaz opalescent Cart; 1991 – yellow opalescent Donkey and Cart (different from topaz).

The Fat Goose was produced in crystal. It is 6½" high (to tip of bill) and is 6" long from breast to tip of tail. This guy is solid glass with excellent detail and is very heavy. It had many uses, including a doorstop and bookend. Most of them seen are rough because they were used as a doorstop. They have not been reissued.

Fat Goose. *Crystal. $250.00–300.00.*

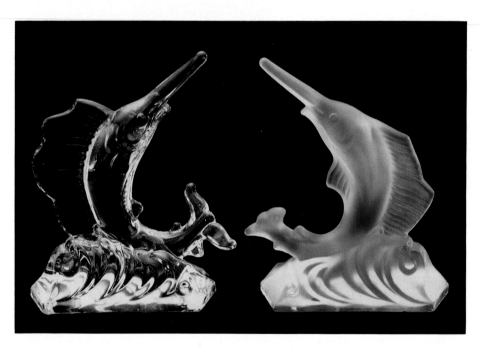

Swordfish. *Crystal, $275.00–325.00. Blue opalescent frosted, $450.00–500.00.*

Duncan produced the Swordfish in three styles. Perhaps different years of production accounts for the variations. The crystal swordfish on the left is also found without spines (lines) in the fins. The swordfish is 5" high and the base is 3¼" long. It was produced in crystal, crystal frosted, blue opalescent, and blue opalescent frosted. It is solid glass and the detail is outstanding. It has not been reissued.

Federal Mirror Bookend. *This bookend is 6¾"*
high and 4¾" wide. It is easily recognized by the
spread-wing eagle on top of the mirror. It has not
been reissued. Rarity prohibits pricing.

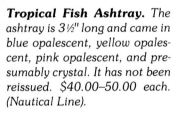
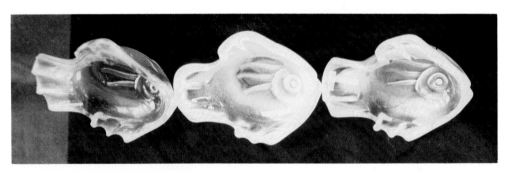

Tropical Fish Ashtray. *The*
ashtray is 3½" long and came in
blue opalescent, yellow opales-
cent, pink opalescent, and pre-
sumably crystal. It has not been
reissued. $40.00–50.00 each.
(Nautical Line).

Tropical Fish Candleholder. *This*
figurine is 5" high and was produced
in crystal, blue opalescent, and pink
opalescent. It has not been reissued.
Crystal, $450.00–500.00. (Sculp-
tured Line).

Duck Smoking Set in Ruby. *7" ruby ashtray, $60.00–80.00. 4" ruby ashtray, $40.00–60.00. 6" ruby cigarette box. $150.00–170.00.*

The Duncan three-piece Duck smoking set consisted of 7" long, 4¾" wide ashtray; 4" long, 2¾" wide ashtray; and 6" long, 4" wide covered cigarette box. It was produced in crystal, ruby, light blue, and perhaps in chartreuse. They are solid glass except the pockets for contents. Detail is good. Some of the crystal items may be found with cranberry or iridescent stains and floral decorations. They were not reissued.

Duck Smoking Items. *4" crystal ashtray as described above. $10.00–20.00. Covered cigarette box. 6", crystal with floral decoration. $50.00–70.00. 4" ruby ashtray as described above. $40.00–60.00.*

Solid Back Swans. *Duncan made the solid back swans in three sizes, 3" long x 2¾" high, 5" long x 4¾" high, and 7" long x 6½" high. They are solid glass and have very little detail. They were not reissued. 7", $65.00–85.00. 5", $25.00–35.00. 3", $15.00–25.00.*

Duncan produced the Pall Mall Swan in 3½", 6", 7", 10½", and 12". Some had candle sockets in the center, obviously part of a console set. They were produced in crystal, crystal engraved and multiple colors including ruby, teakwood, smokey avocado, biscayne green, chartreuse, opal, milk, frosted, and blue. Opal, milk, frosted, and engraved are considered rare. They have molded bodies with applied necks. They were reissued by Tiffin Glass Company in crystal, twilight, milk, greenbriar, desert red, wisteria, cobalt, and pink.

Open Back Swan. *Blue, $70.00–90.00.*

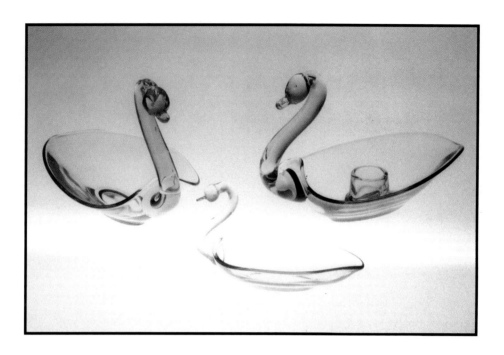

Open Back Swans. *Chartreuse. 7" swan, $35.00–45.00. 3½" swan, $25.00–30.00. 7" candleholder, $45.00–55.00.*

Open Back Swans. *Ruby. 7" candleholder, $65.00–75.00. 12" swan, $85.00–95.00. 7" swan, $45.00–55.00.*

Open Back Swans. *Crystal with engraving. 7" crystal engraved, $65.00–75.00. 7" crystal engraved, $65.00–75.00. 3½" crystal swan, $10.00–15.00.*

Note: The 3½" and 6" crystal open back swan was made with a raised inscription in the bottom "Genuine Duncan" and given away by the company as souvenirs. They are rare.

The Sylvan Swan was produced in 3", 5½", 7½", and 12". The 12" is 10½" high and 11½" wide. They were made in crystal, blue opalescent, yellow opalescent, and pink opalescent. They were not reissued.

Sylvan Swan. *Crystal, 12". $65.00–85.00.*

Sylvan Swans. *Blue opalescent, 5 ½", $65.00–75.00. Yellow opalescent, 7 ½", $95.00–110.00. Pink opalescent, 5 ½", $85.00–95.00.*

These "spread-wing" swans are 11" wide (wing tip to wing tip) and 10" high (to top of neck). They were produced in crystal, blue opalescent, yellow opalescent, and pink opalescent. It is reported that Duncan made these as a special order for Weil-Freeman Company. They are sometimes referred to as WF. Although they have not been reissued, there is however a look-alike which was reportedly made in Czechoslovakia. They are much smaller than the Duncan swan, but to make it even more confusing, they have been seen in yellow opalescent, blue opalescent, pink opalescent, and green opalescent.

Sylvan Swan. *Crystal. $55.00–65.00.*

#1618 Elephant Flower Bowl. *Black satin, 6½" high x 9" long, 1929. Very rare. $400.00 to market.*

Other opaque colors: Teal blue, $350.00–400.00. Jade green, $350.00–400.00.

Other transparent colors: Crystal, green, amethyst, and rose, $250.00–295.00.

#1618 Elephant Flower Bowl. *Teal blue, 6½" high x 9" long, 1929. $350.00–400.00.*

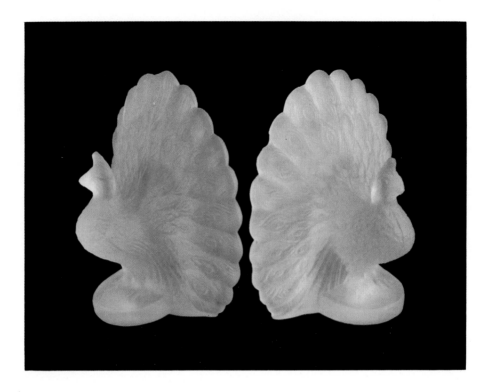

#711 Peacock Bookends. *Very unusual. Crystal satin, 5¾" high. $150.00–175.00 pair.*

Other colors: Black and French opalescent, both rare. $225.00–255.00 pair.

#1565 Turtle Flower Bowl/Aquarium Base. *Rare. Black, 8⅞" long, circa 1929. $175.00–200.00.*

Teal or jade green, $175.00–200.00. Crystal, pink, or green, $95.00–125.00.

Note: This turtle was also made with a lid for a covered bon-bon dish, or, in green only, to accomodate a crystal fish bowl.

#5177 Alley Cat. *Ruby slag, 11" high.*
$55.00–75.00.

Other colors:

1970	Amethyst carnival (original issue)	$75.00–95.00
	Purple slag	55.00–75.00
1985	Velva Rose (ltd. edition 200)	75.00–100.00
	Electric blue carnival	55.00–65.00
	Kelley green iridescent	55.00–65.00
1988/89	Teal marigold	55.00–65.00
1992	Dusty rose iridized for QVC	30.00 (issue price)

Note: See Tiffin, page 188 for design and history of this very famous mold!

#5177 Alley Cat. *11" high. Fenton, electric blue carnival, $55.00–65.00. Tiffin, black satin, $150.00–175.00. Fenton, velva rose, $75.00–100.00.*

Elephant Whiskey Bottle. *Crystal, 8" high, 1935. Printing on bottle reads: "Federal Law Prohibits the Sale or Re-use of this Bottle." This bottle is considered **very rare.** $300.00–325.00.*

Other colors: periwinkle (only one is known), $400.00–450.00.

Elephant Sherry Decanter with Stopper. *Crystal, 9½" high, 1935, no printing. $260.00–285.00.*

#5107 Madonna Prayer Light. *Custard satin, 6" high, 1978. $25.00–35.00.*

1953 introduced Madonna vase in milk glass or blue satin; 1954–57, milk glass only; 1978, blue satin, crystal velvet, custard satin; and 1985, opal glass with decorations and crystal velvet.

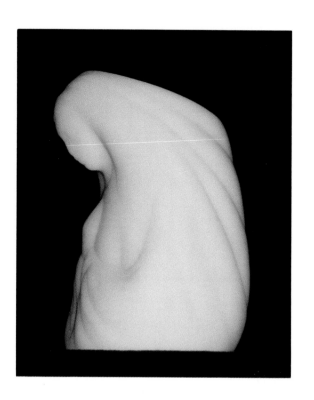

#5156 Fish Vase. *Milk glass with black tail and eyes, 7" high, circa 1953. Rare. $400.00–450.00.*

Other colors: Black with white tail and eyes, and milk glass with black tail, $400.00–450.00.

#5196 Chick on Basket. *Green top with milk glass, 5½" long, 1953–54. $40.00–60.00.*

#5188 Chicken Server. *Milk glass with green, oval shape, 1953–54. Rare. $275.00–300.00.*

Other colors: Milk glass with amethyst.

Note: Made in 1955–56, #5189, in solid milk glass.

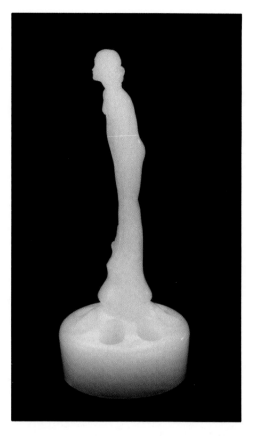

#1645 September Morn Nymph. *Moonstone, with flower frog base, 6¼" high, 1928. $75.00–135.00.*

Note: Peg bottom fits into her special flower frog, candle bowl, or lotus bowl.

#1645 September Morn Nymphs. *Left to right: with flower frog base, 6¼" high, 1928. Ruby, $135.00–165.00. Moonstone, $75.00–135.00. Jade, $75.00–135.00. Pink, $55.00–75.00. Milk glass, $75.00–135.00.*

Note: Mandarin red, Pekin blue, and Chinese yellow (not shown), are <u>very rare</u> and in the $200.00–300.00 range.

#1645 September Morn Nymphs.
*Left to right: with flower frog base, 6¼"
high, 1928. Cobalt, $135.00–165.00.
Dark green, $55.00–75.00. Aquamarine,
$135.00–165.00. Crystal, $45.00–
55.00.*

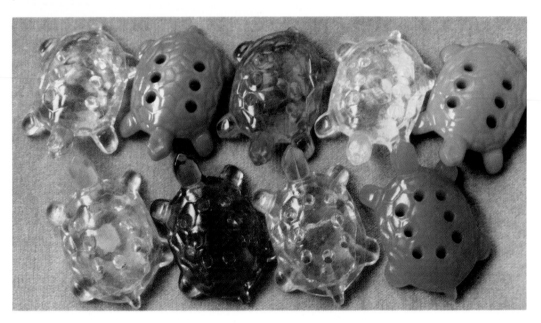

#1564 Turtle Flower Block. *4" long.*

*Top Row: Left to right: Northwood Turtle Flower Block, 6 holes. Crystal, coral, blue, vaseline, opaque
blue.*

*Bottom Row: Fenton, circa 1929, 8 holes. Transparent green, $35.00–55.00. Transparent amethyst,
$55.00–85.00. Transparent pink, $35.00–55.00. Jade, $85.00–95.00.*

Colors not shown: Crystal, $35.00–55.00. Vaseline, $55.00–85.00. Celeste blue, $55.00–85.00.

*Early 1920's colors – rare: Mandarin red, Pekin blue, black, Mongolian green, periwinkle blue.
$95.00–135.00 each.*

*Note: When Northwood went out of business, Fenton purchased the turtle mold and added
2 extra holes. Northwood's colors and prices would match those of Fenton.*

New Souvenir Item. *1990–91 reissue of September Morn Nymph with #9193 Mini Arranger base (flower/candle). Peachaline with black arranger and roseline with opal arranger.*

Note: Both sets were made in limited production and sold for $65.00 per set when issued. Specifically produced for Fenton Art Glass Collectors of America.

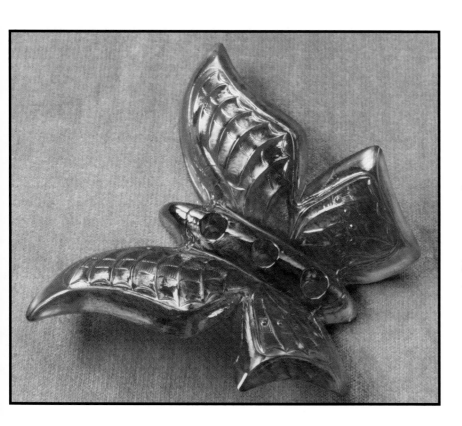

1989 Fenton Souvenir Issue. *Butterfly candleholder, ruby carnival, 7½" long with 5" body containing three candle sockets. $75.00–85.00.*

Note: Frosted ruby carnival issued in 1992. Issue price, $50.00.

Fostoria Glass Company
Moundsville, West Virginia

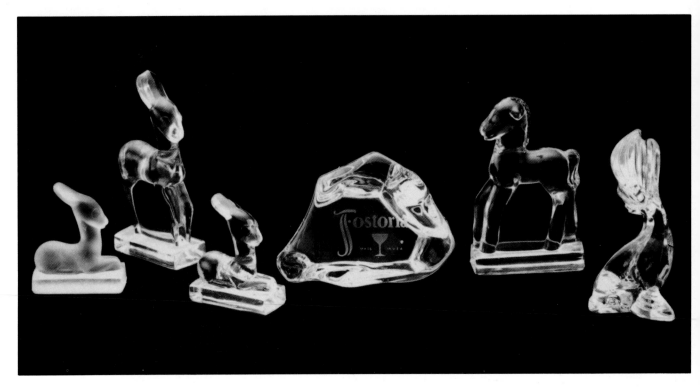

2589½ Deer Reclining. *Silver mist, 2⅜" high, 1940–43. $35.00–45.00.*
2589 Deer Standing. *Crystal, 4¼" high, 1940–43. Also made in silver mist. $35.00–45.00.*
Fostoria Logo.
2589½ Deer Reclining. *Crystal 2⅜" high, 1940–43. $35.00–45.00.*
2589 Colt Standing. *Crystal, 3⅞" high, 1940–43. Also made in silver mist. $35.00–45.00.*
2633B Goldfish. *Crystal, vertical, 4" high, 1950–57. $85.00–95.00.*

Note: Both the reclining and the standing deer were made in milk glass 1954–58. Both colts were reissued in 1977 in blue for Blue Colt Collectibles (1,000 limited edition).

The Fostoria Glass Company was first established in Fostoria, Ohio, in 1887, moving to Moundsville, West Virginia in 1891. Fine handmade glassware was produced by Fostoria. The early 1920's saw the introduction of colors such as canary, green, amber, blue, and ebony. These were followed by orchid, azure blue, pink, and topaz. 1930's colors would add gold tint, empire green, regal blue, burgundy, and ruby. In 1937, in honor of their Golden Jubilee, Fostoria renamed their topaz color "gold-tint."

In 1983 Fostoria was purchased by Lancaster–Colony, and in 1986 the plant was closed. Some animal/figurine production is still being done from old Fostoria molds, for sale through their 11 outlet stores across the country. These reissues are noted within this chapter.

#2589 Standing Deer. *Blue, with Fostoria label, 4⅜"*
high, 1980. $35.00–45.00.

Note: *Made exclusively for Blue Colt*
Collectibles.

#2633A Goldfish. *Horizontal,*
4" long, 1950–57. Very scarce.
$125.00–150.00.

Small Bird Candleholders. *Crystal, 1½" high, internal glass knobs to hold candles,*
signed "Fostoria." $10.00–15.00 each.
Crystal Bear and Owl. *2½" high, current issue.*

Note: *Like #2521 almond/salt dips, made in burgundy, empire green, regal*
blue, and ruby, 1935–42; crystal, 1975–79; milk glass 1954–58; and ruby,
1981–82.

Two-Piece Squirrel Set. *2631/702"A", sitting, amber, 1965–73. $25.00–35.00. 2631/703"B", running, amber, 1965–73. $25.00–35.00.*

Original issue: crystal, 1950–58. Other colors: cobalt, 1965–70; olive green (plain or frosted), 1965–73.

Note: Reported in milk glass, some with gold trim, sitting only.

2632/404 Mama Duck. *Crystal, 4" high, 1950–57. $15.00–25.00.*
2632/405 Duckling. *Head back, "A," amber, 2½", 1965–73. $10.00–15.00.*
2632/405 Duckling. *Head back, "A," cobalt blue, 2½", 1965–70. $20.00–25.00.*
2632/406 Duckling. *Walking, "B," amber, 2⅜", 1965–73. $10.00–15.00.*

Other colors: Olive green, silver mist, light blue, in plain or frosted colors.

Not shown: 2632/407 Duckling, head down, "C," 1½". $15.00–20.00.

Note: Reported in milk glass and ruby. Reissued in 1990 for Fostoria Glass Company outlet stores in crystal only. Reissued in 1991 for Fostoria Glass Company outlet stores in emerald green.

2821/410 Dolphin. *Blue, 4¾", 1971–73. $20.00–25.00.*
2821/420 Frog. *Lemon, 1⅞", 1971–73. $25.00–35.00.*

Other colors: Crystal and olive green (plain or frosted).

*2821/628 Mama Rabbit. Light blue, 2⅛" high, 1971–73. $25.00–35.00.
2821/627 Baby Rabbit. Light blue, 1¼" high, 1971-73. $15.00–20.00.
2821/357 Cat. Light blue, 3¾" high, 1971–73. $25.00–35.00.*

Other colors: Crystal, lemon, olive green (plain or frosted).

*Note: Miniatures not shown: 2821/304 Stork, 2" high, $15.00–20.00. 2821/452
Ladybug, 1¼" high, $15.00–20.00. 2821/527 Owl, 2¾" high, $15.00–20.00. Same
time frame, same colors.*

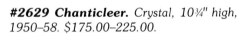

*#2629 Chanticleer. Crystal, 10¾" high,
1950–58. $175.00–225.00.*

*Other colors: Ebony, 1954–57; some deco-
rated; and experimental milk glass.*

#2629 Chanticleer. *Milk glass, 10¾" high. Very rare. $600.00 to market.*

Note: As the milk glass roosters exploded when taken from the molds, FEW survived. In order to save the milk glass production, mold changes were made, making the top tail feathers solid rather than split.

#2629 Chanticleer. *Ebony, 10¾" high, 1953–57. $400.00–600.00.*

#2580 Elephant Bookend. *Crystal, 6½" high, 1940–43. $45.00–65.00.*

Other colors: Silver mist, 1939–43; ebony, 1980 (sold through outlet stores).

Note: Reissued in 1990 in crystal only for Fostoria outlet stores.

#2564 Rearing Horse Bookends. *Crystal, 7¾" high, 1939–58. $35.00–45.00.*

Other colors: Silver mist, 1939–43; ebony (few sold in outlet stores), 1980.

Note: Reissued in 1991 in crystal only for Fostoria outlet stores. See comparison sheet, page 231. Lamps have also been made from this design.

#2531 Polar Bear. *Crystal, 4⅝" high, 1935–44. $55.00–65.00*
#2531 Pelican. *Crystal, 3⅞" high, 1935–44. $55.00–65.00.*

Other colors: Topaz, 1935–36; silver mist, 1936–43; gold tint, 1937–39. $100.00–125.00 each. (Topaz was introduced in 1929 and was changed to gold tint in 1937.) Gold tint, $100.00–125.00.

Note: The pelican was introduced at the 1987 convention by The Fostoria Glass Society of America as "Mascot." See pages 82 and 83 for commemorative issues.

#2531 Penguin. *Crystal, 4⅝" high, 1935–43. $65.00–75.00.*
#2531 Seal. *Crystal, 3⅞" high, 1935–43. $55.00–65.00.*

Other colors: Topaz, 1935–36; gold tint, 1937–39; silver mist, 1936–43.

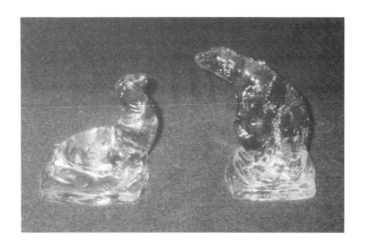

#2531 Seal. *Topaz, 3⅞" high, 1935–36. $100.00–125.00.*
#2531 Polar Bear. *Topaz, 4⅝" high, 1935–36. $100.00–125.00.*

#2531 Penguin. *Topaz, 4⅝" high, 1935–36. $100.00–125.00.*

Cardinal Head. *Silver mist, solid, 6½" high. $100.00–125.00.*

Note: The cardinal head was made for the Car Club Collectors as a radiator ornament. It fits the metal cap of the Model A and the Model T. Also made by Fenton. See page 60.

#2615 Owl Bookend. *Crystal, 7½" high. Made for one year only, 1943. $150.00–175.00 each.*

Other colors: A few were made in ebony in 1980 and sold through the outlet stores.

#2585 Eagle Bookend. *Crystal, 7½" high, 1940–43. $85.00–95.00 each.*

Made in silver mist 1939–43.

#2601 Lyre Bookend. *Crystal, 7" high, Regency pattern, 1942–44. $50.00–75.00 each.*

Also made in silver mist.

Note: Matching console bowl and candleholders were made.

#2634 Mermaid. *Crystal, 11½" high, 1950–58. $100.00–125.00.*
#2641 Sea Horse Bookend. *Crystal, 8" high, on base of waves, 1950–58. $100.00–125.00.*

Note: Do not confuse with the "unknown" seahorse on a scalloped shell. See page 212.

#2497½ Seafood Cocktail Creamer. *Empire green, 3¼" high, (note spout), 1934–40. $45.00–55.00*
#2497 Flying Fish Vase. *Teal green, 7" high, 1965. $25.00–35.00. Also in wisteria, $65.00–75.00; and ruby, $55.00–65.00.*
#2497 Seafood Cocktail. *Crystal, 3¼" high, 1934–40. $20.00–25.00. Also in burgundy, empire green, royal blue, silver mist, and ruby, $30.00–40.00 each.*

Reprinted courtesy of Antique Publications, *Marietta, Ohio.*

Left to right:

#2626 Chinese Lute Figurine. *Ebony wtih gold, 12½" high, 1953–57. Paired with Chinese Lotus Figurine. $600.00–700.00 pair.*
#2626 Chinese Lotus Figurine. *Ebony with gold, 12¼" high, 1953–57. $600.00–700.00 pair.*
#2298 Chinese "Buddha" Bookend. *Ebony with gold trim. 7½" high, 1953–57. $500.00–550.00 pair.*

Other colors: Lute and Lotus, crystal or silver mist, $300.00–500.00 pair.

Left to right:

#2635/471 Madonna. *Crystal, 10" high, 1950's. $45.00–55.00.*
#2635/471 Madonna. *Silver mist, 10" high, 1950's, (black glass lighted bases optional). $45.00–55.00 without base.*
#1 Madonna. *Heisey by Imperial, marked "IG," crystal, 9" high. $35.00–45.00.*

See page 116 for other Imperial colors.

Note: Fostoria also made a 4" Madonna, frosted and pencil slim. The 2635/471 Fostoria Madonna appeared in Tiara's catalogs after 1978. The 2797/473 Fostoria Sacred Heart Madonna, 11½" high, has also been reissued.

#2715/469 St. Francis. *Silver mist, 13½" high, 1957–73. Original, $300.00–350.00.*
#2798/472 Madonna & Child. *Silver mist (black glass lighted bases optional), 13½" high, 1967–73. $200.00–300.00.*

Note: The base on some of the original issue of St. Francis had an irregular triangular shape, while others had a round base. St. Francis was reissued for Lancaster Colony, 1990, in silver mist (with a round base) and sold through Fostoria outlet stores.

Commemorative Pelican. *Amber, 1987. $35.00–45.00.*
Commemorative Pelican. *Pink, 1991. $45.00–55.00.*

Note: 1992 Commemorative Pelican is Raspberry Ice. Issue price is $25.00.

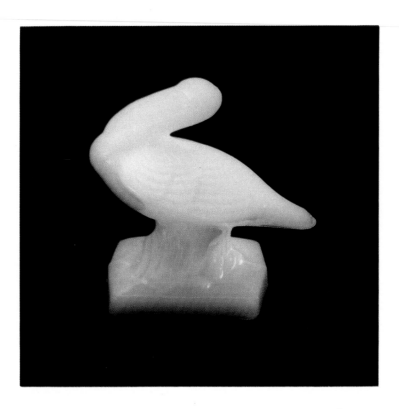

Commemorative Pelican. *Opal/opal iridescent, 1988. $35.00–45.00.*

Commemorative Pelican. *Cobalt blue, 1989. $100.00–125.00.*

Commemorative Pelican. *Depression green, 1990. $65.00–75.00.*

Note: This pelican has a card around its neck stating "Tenth Anniversary 1980–1990 Fostoria Glass Society."

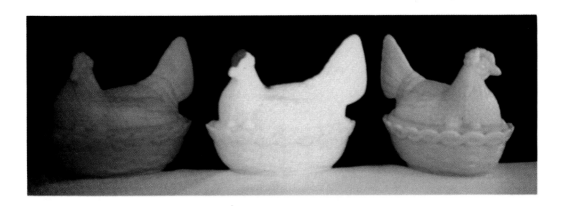

Two-Piece Covered Hen. *Aqua, decorated milk glass and pink, 1960's. $100.00–125.00 each.*

Note: The only covered animal dish ever made by Fostoria.

K.R. Haley Glassware Company
Greensburg, Pennsylvania

Born in 1905, K.R. Haley came from a family of consummate glass designers, beginning with his grandfather, Jonathan, followed by his father, Reuben. Kenneth's father was a master perfectionist and demanded no less from his son! Together their expertise became well known and in high demand.*

Kenneth came to Greensburg in 1934 to do mold work for Overmeyer Mould of Pennsylvania, becoming vice-president in 1937. Two years later, with Herman Lowerwitz as partner, Kenneth Haley started the General Glassware Company of Greensburg, Pennsylvania.

To clear up any confusion in relation to the pieces attributed to K.R. Haley, he designed, or made the models from which the actual molds were created, lending his expertise in the making of the mold. American Glass Company of Carney, Kansas (affiliate of General Glassware), then produced the items in glass, which were sold and distributed through General Glass Company. Mr. Haley was never a manufacturer of glass, but a superb creative artist!

When Herman Lowerwitz, president of American Glass Company, passed away, Mr. Haley dissolved his partnership in General Glassware and incorporated under his own name. His company was in business until 1972 when the corporation was dissolved. (Kemple Glass acquired possession of a number of Mr. Haley's designs.)

Mr. Fred Bickenheuser tells us that the U.S. Glass/Tiffin/Fenton 11" cat was designed by Reuben Haley and his son Kenneth in the 1900's. See page 188 for further cat history.

*For an excellent source of information on the Haley Design Dynasty, see Phoenix and Consolidated Art Glass by Jack D. Wilson.

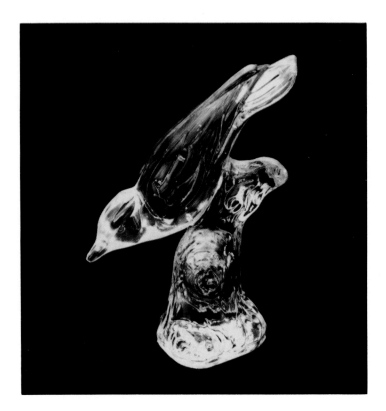

Bird (Robin on Stump). *Crystal, 6" high, 1945–60's, also made in frosted. $10.00–20.00.*

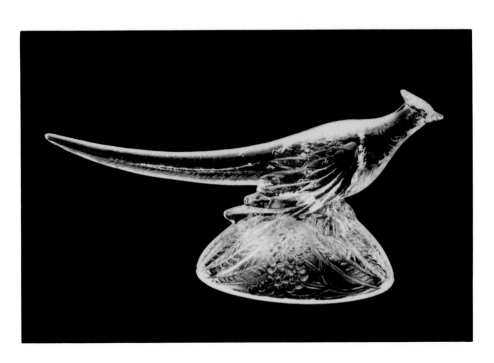

Ringneck Pheasant. *Crystal, 11½" high, hollow base, 1947, also made in frosted. $20.00–25.00.*

Three Ducks Swimming. *Crystal, 9½" long, later produced in frosted. $35.00–45.00.*

Note: Documented as becoming a night light with the addition of a wooden base with bulb.

Small Donkey with Cart. *Crystal. $5.00–15.00.*
Large Donkey with Cart. *Crystal, 4½" high, also made in milk glass. $10.00–20.00.*

Note: Reproductions on this item, in almost every color, are far too numerous to document.

Jumping Horse. *Crystal, 9½" long by 7½" high, hollow base, 1947. $45.00–55.00.*

Haley Rooster. *Head down, crystal, 9" high, hollow base. $25.00–35.00.*
Kemple Rooster. * *Head down, amber, 9" high, hollow base. $25.00–35.00.*
Kemple Rooster. *Head down, milk glass decorated, 9" high, hollow base. $45.00–55.00.*

John E. Kemple purchased the Haley rooster mold. Kemple Glass was produced in the late 1940's and early 1950's, in East Palestine, Ohio, and from the late 1950's through the 1970's in Kenova, West Virginia. Kemple Glass produced this rooster in milk glass, crystal and colors, some were decorated.

Note: The Paden City rooster (head down) is almost identical to the Haley/Kemple rooster, but it is solid glass. See page 171.

Bird (Thrush). *Original Haley issue: crystal or frosted, 1947. $10.00–20.00.*

Shown here is the original Haley mold produced by L.E. Smith in their amberina color. L.E. Smith has produced this bird in several colors and finishes over the years, including a color they called "Alexandrite." In 1980, the Thrush was produced in "Almond Nouveau."

Llama. *A.k.a. Sitting Fawn, crystal, 6" high, also made in frosted glass with hand-painted eyes and nose. $10.00–20.00.*

Note: Kemple Glass bought this mold, also producing it in colors and milk glass.

Trail's End Indian and Pony. *Crystal, 7½" high, 1946.*

Note: Price cannot be determined on this figurine due to its scarcity. However, we felt it was a treasure to share with our readers!

Horse & Rider Bookend. *(Lady Godiva), crystal, 6" high, also made in frosted. $35.00–45.00 each.*

Note: Also seen as a night light, in frosted green.

Victorian Boy and Girl Bookends. *Crystal, 5½" high.*

Note: Due to their small stature, these bookends may have been for children's books.

From a Private Collection.

Pacemaker Ashtray. *Crystal, 3½" high.*

Other colors: Fired Mellotint colors in red, light amber, or apple green; fired Chinese red, green, pink and blue, with black Pacemaker colt in center. $10.00–15.00.

Note: Produced by Knox Glass Company, later by American Glass in the early 1940's, this little ashtray was selected by Randolph Hearst to be given out to tourists as a souvenir of their visit to Hearst Castle. In May 1974, these were sold at the Roosevelt Raceway in New York. The mold is now in the possession of Reikes Crystal, but has not been reproduced.

Heisey Glass Company
Newark, Ohio

Goose Decanter Stopper. *This stopper goes with the Goose Decanter. The decanter was produced in two sizes, 11¾" high and 13½" high. There is a tail approximately ¾" from the bottom of the decanter. This tail extends upwards 1¾". Although all the decanters are all crystal, the stopper and tail also came in frosted. Complete decanter, small, $200.00–250.00; large, $250.00–300.00.*

Heisey Cabachon Advertising Sign. *This advertising sign was produced in the late 1940's and distributed to stores selling Heisey for use in windows and on shelves.*

Penguin Decanter Stopper. *The Penguin Decanter came in two sizes, one pint and one quart. Rolls of glass, decreasing in size as they extend upwards on the decanter depict wings. They extend upwards 1" from the bottom. Complete decanter: pint, $200.00–250.00; quart, $225.00–275.00.*

The Heisey Glass Company was founded during the mid 1890's, in Newark, Ohio, by A.H. Heisey, the son-in-law of George Duncan, owner of the George Duncan & Sons Glass Company. The Heisey Glass Company produced excellent quality handmade glass from 1896 to 1957. Heisey registered the now famous Diamond H as a trademark and started marking glassware with it in 1902. Application of this logo to much of the glassware continued throughout the life of the Heisey Company. Some of the glass was not marked and was sold with a paper label which bore the name "Heisey" and the Diamond H.

After the Heisey factory closed, Imperial Glass Company of Bellaire, Ohio, bought the existing molds. Imperial produced a number of animals in crystal between 1964 and 1967, and again in the later years in both crystal and color, before they closed in 1984.

In 1971, the Heisey Collectors of America, Inc., was formed in Newark, Ohio. This national non-profit organization is dedicated to the study and preservation of Heisey Glass. In 1985, this organization purchased all existing Heisey molds in the Imperial factory except one line, the Old Williamsburg pattern. The purchase price for this line was considered too high and H.C.A. de-

clined. The Heisey molds, including the existing animal molds, are now under the control of H.C.A. They have a Board policy not to make items in the same color as originally made by Heisey. In addition each item made has a non-removable mark, generally HCA and the year.

In 1937, Heisey produced the first animal, the Horse Head bookend. Later, Royal Hickman, a well-known ceramic designer was commissioned to design figurines for Heisey. He designed most of the Heisey animals. His extraordinary talent is reflected in these creations.

A question most often asked by collectors is "How do I tell the difference in crystal animals produced by Imperial from those produced by Heisey?" The late Clarence Vogel, a pioneer in literature on Heisey, was a firm believer that a black light would show the difference between Heisey and Imperial crystal glass. Mr. Vogel's theory contends that under a black light Heisey animals will have yellow tones while those made by Imperial will reflect only the color of the light. We have experimented wtih this and found it to be true on the items tested.

Measurements of items in this chapter were actually taken from the figurines pictured. Measurements will vary with any item whose base or bottom has been factory finished by polishing or grinding smooth.

Flying Mare. *Amber. 9" high, 12" long, 1951–52. When marked, it appears on base, left side under flanks. $2,200.00–3,000.00.*

Other colors: Crystal and crystal frosted.

Reissues: Imperial Glass Company, in crystal and colors. See page 138.

Note: This figurine is solid glass. This magnificent piece is the largest of the Heisey animals. It is one of the most desirable and demands the highest of prices.

Filly, Head Backward. *Crystal, 8⅛"
high, 5¼" long (from front to back at
base), 1948–49. Mark appears on lower
abdomen, left side. $1,100.00–
1,400.00.*

*Reissues: Imperial Glass Company, in
crystal and multiple colors. See page
138.*

*Note: This figurine is solid glass
and has excellent detail. This filly
is more difficult to find and demands a higher price than the head
forward filly.*

Filly, Head Forward. *Crystal, 8½"
high, 5¼" long (from front to back at
base), 1948–49. Mark appears on the
side of the right front leg, 1" above base.
$800.00–1,000.00.*

*Reissues: Imperial Glass Company, in
crystal and multiple colors. See page
130.*

*Note: This figurine is solid glass and like the head backward filly, has good detail. Although the fillies
were made for the same period of time, the head forward filly is seen more often.*

Clydesdale. *Crystal, 7½"high, 7"long
(front to back at base), 1942–48. Seldom marked, but when found, the
mark appears on the extreme lower
right back leg. $300.00–400.00.*

*Other colors: Crystal frosted and am-
ber.*

*Reissues: Imperial Glass Company, in
multiple colors. See page 125.*

*Note: This figurine is solid glass.
He has excellent detail and very
large hooves.*

Show Horse. *Crystal, 7⅜" high, 7½"
long (farthest points), 1948–49. Mark
appears on the side of the left rear leg, 1" above base. $1,000.00–1,500.00.*

Other colors: Crystal frosted.   *Reissues: Imperial Glass Company, in crystal and amber. See page 138.*

*Note: This figurine is solid glass and has excellent detail. It was supposedly modeled after Mr. Heisey's
horse, "Goodness Gracious."*

Clydesdale. *Amber. Rarity prohibits pricing.*

This amber Clydesdale is still on the bust-off as it came out of the mold. Because of its poor quality it should have been destroyed (remelted) but obviously some worker wanted it and took it home with them. Notice the mold did not fill completely and the mane is partially missing. This guy is a beautiful light amber and stands proudly in the Heisey Museum in Newark, Ohio. He was purchased in an auction by a Heisey Study Club and donated to the Museum.

Plug Horse. *Crystal, 4" high, 4" long (tip of nose to back of base), 1941–46. When marked, the mark appears between the front legs. $95.00–135.00.*

Other colors: Crystal frosted, amber, and cobalt.

Reissues: Imperial Glass Company in crystal and color. Has been made by Imperial, Viking, and Fenton for Heisey Collectors Of America, Inc., as convention souvenirs since 1977. See pages 141–143.

Note: This figurine is solid glass and has fair detail. This guy is not handsome. The one on the left was painted by a decorating company. Those in amber and cobalt are rare. Sometimes referred to by other names such as Oscar and Sparky. See page 135.

Donkey. *Crystal, 6½" high, 5" long (from extended upper lip to hind hooves), 1944–53. When marked, the mark appears on the left hind leg above the hoof. $225.00–300.00.*

Other colors: Crystal frosted.

Reissues: Imperial Glass Company, in crystal and colors. See pages 132 and 134.

Note: This figurine is solid glass and has excellent detail. It is sometimes seen decorated with bright colors like the plug horse.

Colt, Kicking. *Crystal, 4" high, 3½" long (tip of ear to back of base), 1941– 45. When marked, the mark appears behind the legs. $165.00–195.00.*

Other colors: Amber and cobalt.

Reissues: Imperial Glass Company, in crystal and multiple colors. See pages 127, 128, and 135.

Note: This figurine is solid glass and has excellent detail. Also referred to as kicking pony. The head and face on all three colts have the same appearance and detail.

Colt, Standing. *Crystal, 5" high, 3" long (front of head to tip of tail), 1940–52. When marked, the mark appears on the right side between legs near the base. $65.00–95.00.*

Other colors: Amber and cobalt.

Reissues: Imperial Glass Company, in crystal and multiple colors. See pages 127, 128, and 135.

Note: This figurine is solid glass and has excellent detail. This colt was produced for approximately eight years longer than the other two, therefore, it is quite common and seen often. It is often confused with the Paden City colt. See page 169 for comparison.

Colt, Balking. *Crystal, 3½" high, 3½" long (tip of tail to front of base), 1941–45. When marked, the mark appears between the legs on the left side. $165.00–195.00.*

Other colors: Amber and cobalt.

Reissues: Imperial Glass Company, in crystal and multiple colors. See pages 127 and 128.

Note: This figurine is solid glass and has excellent detail. Like the kicking and standing colts, this one stands on a rectangular glass base. Like the kicking colt, the balking colt gives an almost playful appearance. See page 128 for ruby issue.

Colt, Standing. *See above for details. This figurine is cobalt and is extremely rare and very expensive. $800.00–1,000.00.*

Colt, Standing. *This figurine in amber is rare and expensive. It is seen more often in amber than cobalt. $500.00–600.00.*

Rearing Horse Bookend. *Crystal, 7½" high, 6½" long (at the base), 1940's. Not marked. $800.00–1,000.00.*

Reissues: Imperial Glass Company, in colors. See page 138.

Note: This figurine is solid glass except under the rear feet and tail which is hollow. Detail is good; however, the quality is only fair. This figurine is extremely rare and demands an equivalent price. Obviously there were only a limited quantity made as they were not a Heisey catalog listed item. The head is raised and looks straight ahead, this alone makes it easily identified when compared to figurines made by other companies. See page 231 for comparison with other Rearing Horse bookends.

Horse Head Bookend. *A value is yet to be established on this set of bookends.*

We do not advocate this horse head bookend as being Heisey, however, molds were found with Heisey animal molds in the Imperial factory when Heisey Collectors of America purchased the molds. The molds carried the same number found in Heisey records for a horse head bookend. It has been reported that they were made also by Corning Glass in Pittsburgh. The glass is very poor quality, except for a pair on display in the Heisey Museum, which appears to be better quality. We saw one pair which had a label from Ovington's, Fifth Avenue, New York. Where was Ovington's getting them? Certainly not from Heisey based on the quality as compared to other Heisey animals.

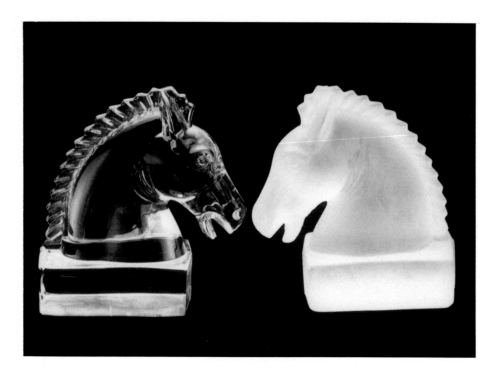

Horse Head Bookend. *Crystal and crystal frosted, 6⅞" high, 6¼" long (nose to mane), 1937–55. Seldom marked, but when marked it appears on the side of the neck, immediately above the base. Crystal, $90.00–120.00; frosted, $75.00–100.00.*

Other colors: Amber.   Reissues: None.

Note: This figurine is solid glass and is very heavy. This was the first of what is considered Heisey animals. It has excellent detail.

Horse Head Bookend. *Amber. Details of this bookend can be found with the preceding photo. This animal is extremely RARE. Rarity prohibits pricing.*

Chicken Family.

Rooster. *Crystal, 5½" high, 5" long (breast to farthest most point of tail), 1948–49. Seldom marked, but when found, the mark appears on the right side, tip of first feather. $300.00–375.00.*

Other colors: Crystal frosted and amber.

Reissues: Imperial Glass Company, milk glass, and amber. See page 136.

Note: This figurine is solid glass and has good detail. He is standing tall and gives the appearance that he is extremely proud. This animal was only made over a two year period and is not seen too often.

Chick, Head Up. *Crystal, 1" high, 1⅜" long (tip of tail to top of head), 1948–49. Not seen marked by the author. $60.00–80.00.*

Reissues: Imperial Glass Company, in milk glass. See page 136.

Note: This figurine is solid glass and has very little detail. From all appearance the same mold was used for the head up and the head down chick, the difference is the angle of the grinding on the bottom. Same method as used on the sparrow.

Chick, Head Down. *Crystal, 1" high, 1⅜" long (tip of tail to top of head), 1948–49. Although the author has not seen a chick bearing the Heisey mark, a possibility exists that some were marked. $60.00–80.00.*

Reissues: Imperial Glass Company, in milk glass. See page 136.

Note: This figurine is solid glass and has very little detail. It is the smallest of the Heisey figurines. The chicks are sometimes confused with the New Martinsville (Viking) chicks. See page 151. The wings on the Heisey chicks are smooth mounds where the New Martinsville have an actual line outlining the wings.

Hen. *Crystal, 4¼" high, 3¾" long (tip of tail to front of head), 1948–49. Seldom marked but when found, it appears on the right side at the tip of the wing. $325.00–400.00.*

Reissues: Imperial Glass Company, in crystal and multiple colors. See pages 132 and 136.

Note: This figurine is solid glass and detail is good. The detail is actually better than the rooster. Like the rooster and chicks, the hen was only made over a two year period and is not easy to find.

Fighting Rooster. *Crystal, 7½" high, 5½" long (tip of beak to back of tail), 1940–46. Seldom marked, when found, it appears on the right side under the wing. $150.00–200.00 each.*

Other colors: Crystal frosted.

Reissues: Imperial Glass Company, in crystal and color. See page 136.

Note: This figurine is solid glass and has excellent detail; however, the tails are filled with mold marks, perhaps it was difficult to get out of the mold. Because the beak is extended, they are quite often seen chipped or broken.

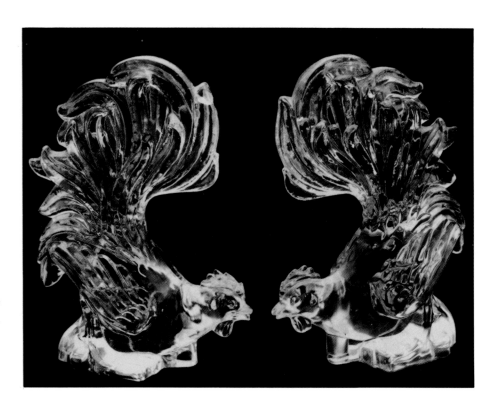

Rooster Vase. *Crystal, 6¼" high, 6" long (front of breast to back of tail), 1939–48. Not marked. $60.00–85.00.*

Other colors: Crystal frosted.

Reissues: None.

Note: This figurine is solid glass except for the back part which forms the vase. A quarter-inch pocket is formed in the base by the outside ridge which it sits on. This guy has excellent detail, even his feet are quite detailed. They have been seen in crystal frosted. Although the figurine was made by Heisey, we are not sure if they were frosted by Heisey or another company.

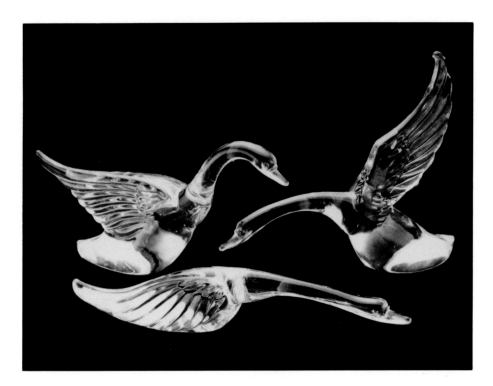

Wings Half. *(Left). Crystal, 4¼" high, 8½" long (tip of tail to tip of bill), 1942–53. When marked, the mark appears midway on left side near the base. $80.00–110.00.*

Other colors: Crystal frosted.

Reissues: Imperial Glass Company, in crystal and color. See page 138.

Note: This figurine is solid glass and has good detail. It is sometimes seen with floral decorations. This goose is seen much more often than the wings up and wings down. Obviously, this one was not as easily broken.

Heisey Geese.

Wings Down. *(Center). Crystal, 2" high, 10¼" long (tip of tail to tip of bill), 1942–53. When marked, it appears on the left side, third feather near the base. $400.00–475.00.*

Other colors: Crystal frosted.

Reissues: None.

Note: This figurine is solid glass and has good detail. The neck was very easily broken which probably accounts for its scarcity.

Wings Up. *(Right). Crystal, 6½" high, 7½" long (tip of tail to tip of bill), 1942–53. When marked, it appears midway on the left side near the base. $80.00–110.00.*

Other colors: Crystal frosted.

Reissues: Imperial Glass Company, in crystal. See page 138.

Note: This figurine is solid glass and has good detail. Because the wings are extended upwards, it is easily knocked over and generally the wing tip will break. Although the wings up is seen more often than the wings down, it is seen less often than the wings half.

Duckling, Standing. *Crystal, 2½"
high, 1¾" long (length of base), 1947–
49. When marked, it appears on the
left side, above the base behind the
feet. $125.00–150.00.*

Other colors: Crystal frosted.

*Reissues: Imperial Glass Company, in
multiple colors. See page 130.*

*Note: This is one of the smaller
Heisey figurines and is solid glass.
It is sometimes referred to as
"Walking Duckling."*

Wood Ducks.

Duckling, Floating. *Crystal, 2¼" high, 3¼" long (overall length), 1947–49. When marked it
appears on the left side below the wing. $140.00–170.00.*

Other colors: Crystal frosted.

Reissues: Imperial Glass Company, in multiple colors. See page 130.

*Note: This is also one of the smaller Heisey figurines and is solid glass. This one has
about the same profile as the mother.*

———

Mother. *Crystal, 4½" high, 6" long (overall length), 1947–49. When marked, it appears on the
left side on the bottom feather. $550.00–625.00.*

Other colors: Crystal frosted.

Reissues: Imperial Glass Company, in crystal and multiple colors. See pages 130 and 133.

Note: This figurine is solid glass and has excellent detail. It is rather difficult to find.

Swan. *Crystal, 7" high, 8½" long (neck to tip of tail), 1947–53. When marked, it appears on the left side, under the wing on the body. $700.00–800.00.*

Other colors: Crystal frosted.

Reissues: Imperial Glass Company, in crystal and colors. See page 138.

Note: This figurine is solid glass. Detail is excellent. Has appeared in several Heisey advertisements.

Cygnet. *Crystal, 2⅛" high, 2½" long (tip of tail to chest), 1947–49. When marked, it appears on the right side under the wing near the base. $150.00–200.00.*

Other colors: Crystal frosted.   *Reissues: Imperial Glass Company, in multiple colors. See page 137.*

Note: This little fellow is solid glass and has good detail. Because of its size, when marked, the mark stands out.

Pouter Pigeon. *Crystal, 6½" high, 7½" long (overall length), 1947–49. Marked left side, ¾" above base, between wing and leg. $500.00–700.00.*

Other colors: Crystal frosted.

Reissues: Imperial Glass Company, in crystal. See page 138.

Note: This elegant figurine is solid glass and has excellent detail. This beautiful bird will enhance any animal collection.

Wings Half. Crystal, 5" high, 5½" long (wing tip to tip of bill), 1947–55. When marked, it appears on the left side near the front, above the base. $175.00–235.00.

Other colors: Crystal frosted.

Reissues: Imperial Glass Company, in crystal and multiple colors. See pages 131 and 134.

Note: This figurine is solid glass and has fair detail. The wings half is seen more often than the wings down but is seen less often than the wings up. It demands a price in the range between the other two.

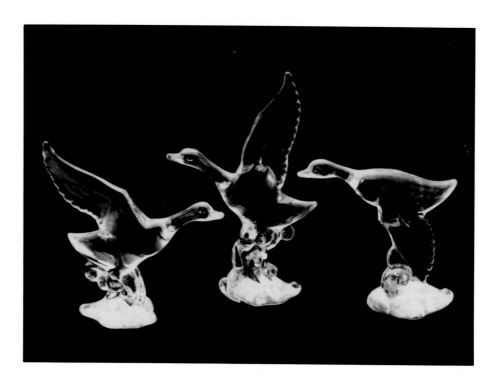

Heisey Mallards.

Wings Up. Crystal, 6¾" high, 4¾" long (tip of bill to tip of tail), 1947–55. When marked, the mark appears on the left side near the front, above the base. $125.00–150.00.

Other colors: Crystal frosted.

Reissues: Imperial Glass Company, in crystal and multiple colors. See pages 131 and 134.

Note: This figurine is solid glass and has fair detail. For some reason the wings up is seen more often than the other two.

Wings Down. Crystal, 4½" high, 4½" long (tip of bill to tip of tail), 1947–55. When marked, it appears on the left side, near the front, above the base. $275.00–325.00.

Other colors: Crystal frosted.

Reissues: Imperial Glass Company, in crystal and multiple colors. See page 131.

Note: This figurine is solid glass and detail is good, somewhat better than the other two. The wings down is seen less often than the other two and demands a much higher price.

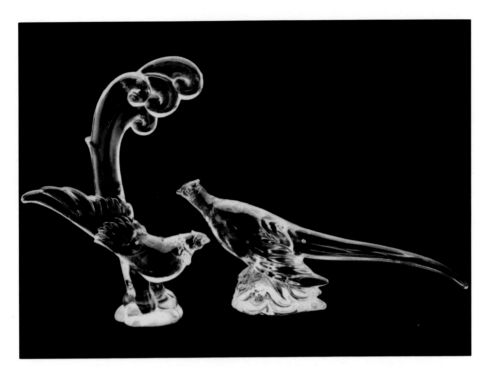

Asiatic Pheasant. *(Left). Crystal, 10½" high, 7½" long (wing tip to beak), 1945–55. Generally marked, mark appears midway on the right side of base. $225.00–300.00.*

Other colors: Crystal frosted.

Reissues: Imperial Glass Company, crystal and color. See page 138.

Note: This figurine is solid glass. The beak is extremely vulnerable and chips easily.

Ringneck Pheasant. *(Right). Crystal, 5" high, 12" long (tip of tail to beak), 1942–53. Seldom marked, but when found, mark appears on left side of base, midway under wing. $110.00–140.00.*

Other colors: Crystal frosted.

Reissues: Imperial Glass Company, in crystal 1964–67, and later in color. See Heisey by Imperial, page 138.

Note: This figurine is solid glass. It is sometimes found with non-Heisey decorations, black, red, gold, and white amplification and sometimes with floral decorations. Heisey did not make "short" tail pheasants; therefore, those found with short tails have been broken and repaired by grinding them smooth.

Sparrow. *Crystal, 2¼" high, 4" long (beak to tip of tail), 1942–45. Not marked. $75.00–100.00.*

Other colors: Crystal frosted.

Reissues: Imperial Glass Company, in color only. See page 138.

Note: This figurine is solid glass and has fair detail. Catalogs indicate three different sparrows, #1, #2, and #3, this can only be attributed to the angle to which the base is ground. One can find many more than three angles to which the base is ground. This angle will also vary the normal 2¼" height of the tail.

Rabbit Paperweight. *Crystal, 2¾" high, 3¾" long (base), 1941–46. Not marked. $100.00–150.00.*

Other colors: Crystal frosted.

Reissues: Produced by Imperial Glass Company in milk glass color and possibly crystal between 1964 and 1967. See page 136.

Note: *This figurine is solid glass including the base. His ears are layed back and he gives the appearance that his eyes are closed. Detail is good.*

Bunny, Head Down. *Crystal, 2½" high, 3" long (tip of tail to front of head), 1948–52. Seldom marked, but if found, mark appears on the left side near the front on the base. $150.00–200.00.*

Other colors: Crystal frosted.

Reissues: None in crystal. Imperial Glass Company in milk glass and other colors, see page 137. By Dalzell/Viking, see page 137.

Note: *This little guy's head is down as if he were eating. He is solid glass and if you look close and use some imagination you can see his feet at the base.*

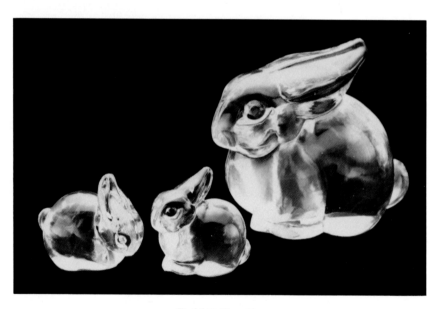

Rabbit Family.

Bunny, Head Up. *Crystal, 2½" high, 2½" long (tip of nose to tail), 1948–49. Seldom marked, but when found, mark appears on the left side near the front on the base. $150.00–190.00.*

Other colors: Crystal frosted.

Reissues: None in crystal. Imperial Glass Company in milk glass and other colors, see page 137. In ruby by Dalzell/Viking, see page 137.

Note: *This little guy's head is up as if he were on watch. He is solid glass and has almost the same profile as the mother rabbit.*

Mother Rabbit. *Crystal, 4½" high, 5½" long (tip of nose to tail), 1948–52. Seldom marked, the mark appears on the left side near the front on the base which is actually the foot. $600.00–800.00.*

Other colors: Crystal frosted.

Reissues: None in crystal. Imperial Glass Company in milk glass and other colors, see page 137.

Note: *This figurine is solid glass and has good detail.*

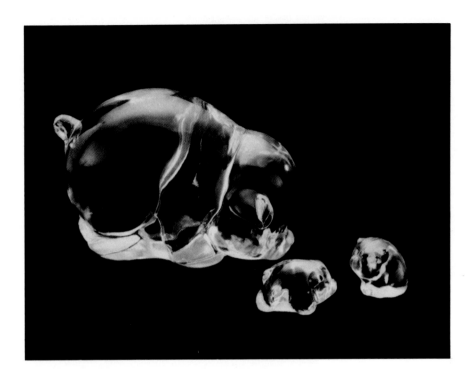

Pig Family.

Sow. *Crystal, 3" high, 4½" long (tip of tail to nose), 1948–49. Seldom marked, mark appears on the right side, near the base between the legs. $450.00–650.00.*

Reissues: Imperial Glass Company, produced in crystal and multiple colors. See page 127.

Note: This figurine is solid glass. She is sometimes confused with the New Martinsville mother pig. To note the differences, see page 152.

Piglet, Walking. *Crystal, ⅞" high, 1½" long (tip to tip), 1948–49. Seldom marked, but when found, it appears on the left side near the base between the legs. $75.00–110.00.*

Reissues: Imperial Glass Company, produced in multiple colors. See page 127.

Note: This figurine is solid glass. Detail is not great. Many times referred to as "standing piglet."

Piglet, Sitting. *Crystal, 1⅛" tall, 1⅛" long (nose to tail), 1948–49. Seldom marked, when found, the mark appears on the right side between the legs. $75.00–110.00.*

Reissues: Imperial Glass Company, produced in multiple colors. See page 127.

Note: This figurine is solid glass. Detail like the other piglet is not great.

Large Elephant (Papa). *Crystal, 5"
high, 6½" long (overall length), 1944–
53. When marked, it appears on the
left side, between the legs near the
base. $325.00–400.00.*

Other colors: Crystal frosted and amber.

*Reissues: Imperial Glass Company,
crystal, amber, and other colors. See
page 138.*

*Note: This figurine is solid glass
and has excellent detail. He has his
trunk raised above his head as if he
is issuing a warning.*

Elephant Family.

Medium Elephant (Mama). *Crystal, 4" high, 6½" long
(overall length), 1944–55. When marked, it appears on the
left side, between the legs near the base. $350.00–425.00.*

Other colors: Crystal frosted and amber.

*Reissues: Imperial Glass Company in crystal and multiple
colors. See pages 132 and 134.*

*Note: This figurine is solid glass. Her trunk is lowered,
curls on the end and forms a loop. Details are about the
same as the large elephant except on a smaller scale.*

Small Elephant (Baby). *Crystal, 4½" high, 5" long (overall
length), 1944–53. When marked, mark appears on the left
side, between the legs near the base. $175.00–225.00*

Other colors: Crystal frosted and amber.

*Reissues: Imperial Glass Company, in crystal and multiple
colors. See page 131.*

*Note: This figurine is solid glass. As if he is imitating his
father, he also has his trunk lifted above his head.*

Middle Elephant (Mama).
Amber. $1,200.00–1,600.00.

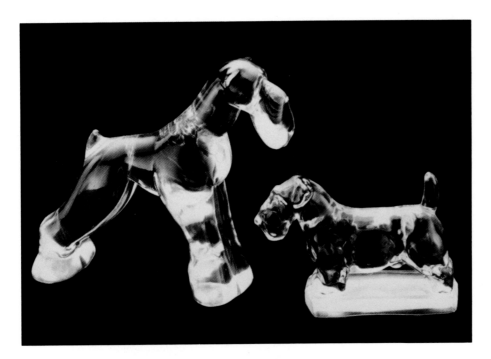

Airedale. Left: Crystal, 5¾" high, 6½" long (farthest most points), 1948–49. Seldom marked, but when found, the mark appears on the side of the left back leg, 1¼" up from the base. $400.00–500.00.

Reissues: Imperial Glass Company, in crystal and multiple colors. See page 126.

Note: This figurine is solid glass and is of excellent quality. Detail is good.

Sealyham Terrier (Scottie). Right: Crystal, 3" high, 4¾" long (farthest points), 1941–46. Seldom marked, but when found, it appears on the side of the body. $75.00–125.00.

Reissues: Imperial Glass Company, in crystal and multiple colors. See page 126.

Note: This figurine is solid glass and stands on a solid glass base. Quality and detail are excellent.

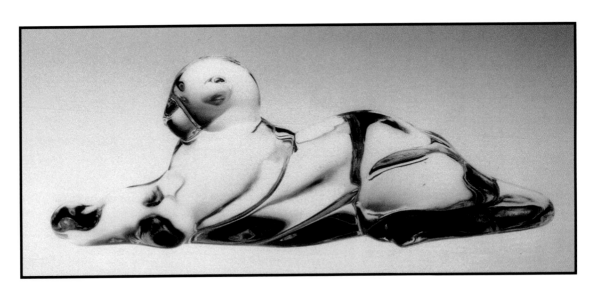

Tiger Paperweight. Crystal, 2¾" high, 8" long, 1949. When marked, it appears near the base, in front of right hind leg. $900.00–1,100.00.

Other colors: Crystal frosted, frosted highlighting.

Reissues: Imperial Glass Company, in crystal and multiple colors. See page 135.

Note: This figurine is solid glass. Detail is fair. The tail is wide and wraps to the left side. He is difficult to find.

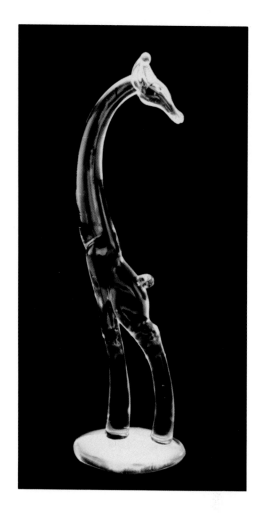

Giraffe. *Crystal, 10¾" high, 3" long (length of base), 1942–52. When marked, it appears on right side of front leg, near the base. $175.00–240.00.*

Other colors: Crystal frosted and amber.

Reissues: Imperial Glass Company, in crystal, amber, and other colors. See page 138.

Note: This figurine is solid glass and has good detail. They were listed in a catalogue as being available in amber, however, they are unseen. The neck was hand-shaped after they were removed from the mold, therefore, the head may be facing different directions and the height may have considerable variances. Some have been seen where the neck had drooped so much that the head gave the appearance that the giraffe was grazing.

Bull. *Crystal, 4" high, 7½" long (tip of tail to front hooves), 1949–52. Mark appears under right front leg on belly near the base. $1,200.00–1,600.00.*

Other colors: Crystal frosted.

Reissues: Imperial Glass Company, in crystal and multiple colors. See page 138.

Note: This figurine is solid glass and has super detail. This guy demands top price in the market.

Doe Head Bookend. *Crystal, 6¼" high, 3¼" wide at bottom, year of production is unknown. Mark appears on the lower left side. $600.00–800.00.*

Other colors: Crystal frosted.

Reissues: None. However, believed to be reproduced in a small quantity in late 1979 or early 1980, in the Ohio area.

Note: This figurine is solid glass and detail is only fair. One has to look close to see that it is in fact a doe's head. From a distance it looks more like a rabbit with its ears up.

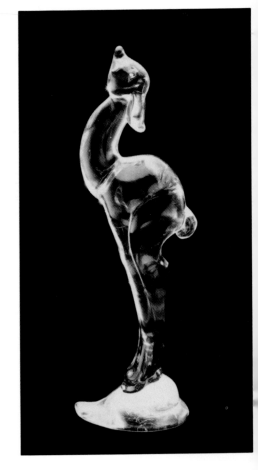

Gazelle. *Crystal, 10¾" high, 3¼" long (length of base), 1947–49. Mark appears on the side of the left hoof. $1,200.00–1,500.00.*

Other colors: Crystal frosted.

Reissues: Imperial Glass Company in crystal and color. See page 129.

Note: This elegant figurine is solid glass and has excellent detail. Was known in certain Heisey circles as the "Constipated Deer." It is sometimes confused by collectors with the Tiffin Fawn, see page 185. Imperial Glass Company produced this animal in cobalt without removing the Diamond H. This has caused a tremendous amount of confusion and many thought this was a Heisey production simply because it had the Heisey mark. The crystal reissue refers to the late Imperial reissue before the factory closed.

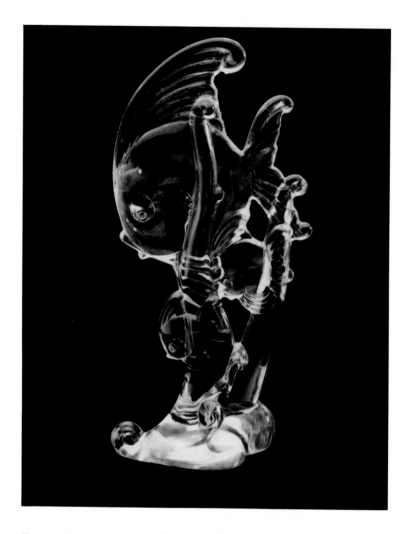

Tropical Fish. *Crystal, 12" high, 6½" long (from front of base to back of seaweed stalk holding top fish), 1948–49. When marked, it appears on the right side, near the bottom of the back stalk of seaweed. $1,400.00–1,700.00.*

Other colors: Crystal frosted.

Reissues: Imperial Glass Company in crystal and color. See page 138.

Note: Figurine is solid glass and has excellent detail. This elegant figurine is the tallest of the Heisey figurines. Lamp companies mounted them on a base for lamps. When one looks close, you can actually see three fish mounted on two stalks of seaweed.

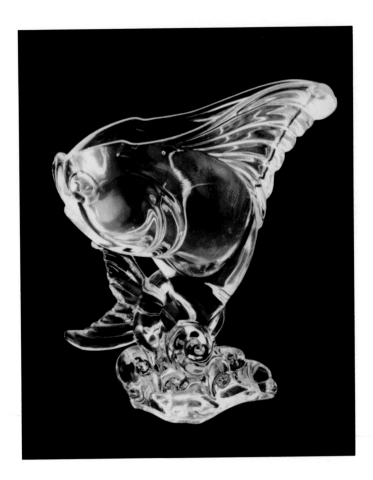

Fish Bowl. *Crystal only, 9½" high, 8½" long (from front to back at the top), 1941–1946. Marked in the middle of the bottom. $350.00–450.00.*

Reissues: None.

Note: The base is solid glass up to the fish which is hollow and holds one pint of liquid. The glass is wavy and has numerous mold marks. Decorating companies decorated them by applying bright colors such as red, gold, white, and black to various features or applied ruby stain. The stain is easily removed.

Fish Bookends. *Crystal, 6½" high, 5" long (from front of base to end of lower fin), 1942–52. When marked, it appears on the left side above the base in the middle. Pair, $175.00–250.00.*

Other colors: Crystal frosted and high-lighted.

Reissues: Imperial Glass Company in multiple colors. See page 137.

Note: These figurines are solid glass with excellent detail. Decorating companies also decorated these guys with bright colors. See page 94 for decorative colors.

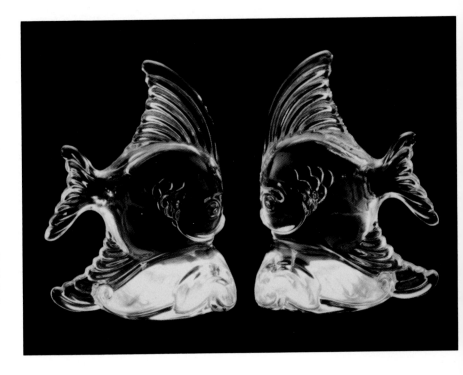

Fish Candlesticks. *(Back). Crystal only, 5" high, 4" long (at the base), 1941–48. Not marked. Pair, $250.00–350.00.*

Reissues: Imperial Glass Company in color. See page 129.

Note: This figurine is solid glass except for the candle socket. The mouth is open which forms the candle socket. The socket is 1⅛" to 1¾" deep from high to low points formed by the mouth. This guy has excellent detail.

Fish Match Holder. *(Front). Crystal only, 3" high, 2¾" long (length at base), 1944–46. Not marked. $125.00–150.00.*

Reissues: Imperial Glass Company in color. See page 129.

Note: This figurine is solid glass except for the pocket formed to hold matches. The fish has his mouth open which forms the pocket. This opening is 1⅛" to 1¼" deep from high to low points formed by the mouth. Detail is excellent.

Heisey made only two figural flower holders, the Kingfisher and the Duck floral block. Both were made from the late 1920's into the early 1930's. These flower holders were made in crystal, Moongleam (green), Flamingo (pink), and Hawthorne (light amethyst).

Duck Floral Block. Hawthorne (left) and flamingo (right), 5" high (including block), 5¼" diameter (block), late 1920's into early 1930's. Not marked. Hawthorne, $175.00–225.00; flamingo, $150.00–200.00.

Other colors: Crystal, moongleam.

Reissues: none.

Note: This is a two-piece item. The duck sits in the block which has 10 holes in the top and bottom rims. Heisey also made a candleholder which fits the block.

Kingfisher. Hawthorne, 5½" high (including base), 4½" diameter (base), late 1920's into early 1930's. Mark appears ¼" in front of right foot (toes). $225.00–275.00.

Other colors: Crystal, moongleam, and flamingo.

Reissues: Imperial Glass Company in black. See page 138.

Note: The Kingfisher is one piece of glass. The base has 10 holes for flowers. He has excellent feather detail and both feet are visible.

Heisey made many animal and figural related items, especially during the 1940's and 1950's, until the factory closed. The next few photos are examples of these related items.

Heisey made several styles of cocktail shakers and more than one size (capacity). These stoppers will fit all of them. The cocktail shakers are unique in that they have a glass strainer that fits into the shaker and then the stopper fits down in the strainer.

All five of the figural stoppers have excellent detail.

Rams Head Stopper. Crystal, 3½" high. Not marked. $125.00–150.00.

Reissues: The Rams Head Stopper was produced in 1979. They were produced in crystal and blue milk. We will not refer to them as a reissue because they were not the same size as the original Heisey stoppers. The reproductions are larger, 3¾" high and 1⅞" in diameter where Heisey was 3½" high and 1⅝" in diameter. The reproductions have a "B" under the back of the right horn. It was called a paperweight.

Figural Cocktail Shaker Stoppers.

Small Horse Head Stopper. Crystal, 4" high. Not marked. $50.00–75.00.

Reissues: The same company that reproduced the Rams Head reproduced the Small Horse Head Stopper, in crystal. Both the Rams Head and Small Horse Head were advertised in the February 1980 Glass Review.

Note: The easiest way to tell the Small Horse Head from the Large Horse Head is the small guy has his ears laid back.

Large Horse Head Stopper. Crystal, 4½" high. Not marked. $100.00–135.00.

Reissues: None.

Note: The ears on this horse are erect and he has more mane showing than the smaller horse head stopper.

Rooster Head Stopper. Crystal, 4½" high. Not marked. $35.00–45.00.

Other colors: Crystal frosted.

Reissues: None.

Note: This is the most common of the figural stoppers. Cocktail glasses were made with this design as the stem.

Girl's Head Stopper. Crystal, 4½" high. Not marked. $175.00–225.00.

Reissues: Imperial Glass Company in amber.

Note: This is the hardest one of the figural stoppers to find, and naturally demands the highest price.

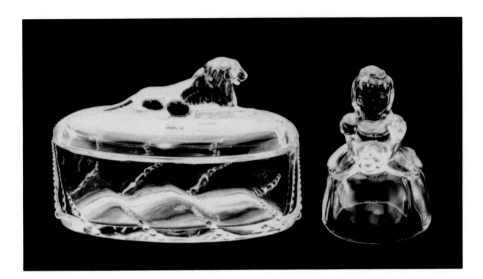

Lion Covered Trinket Box. *Crystal, 4½" high, 6½" long. Marked on the very bottom in the center. $550.00–750.00.*

Reissues: Imperial Glass Company.

Note: This item was produced very late in the life of the Heisey factory and was probably still in production at the time the factory closed. This item is part of the Waverly pattern.

Victorian Bell. *Crystal, 4¼" high, 2¾" diameter (bottom), 1944–48. When marked, it appears on the bustle. $50.00–75.00.*

Other colors: Crystal frosted.

Reissues: Imperial Glass Company.

Note: This little lady is fairly common and is not too difficult to find.

#1 Madonna. *Crystal and crystal frosted, 9" high, 3" square base, 1942–56. When marked, it appears in the center of the back of the base. Crystal, $75.00–125.00; crystal frosted, $65.00–95.00.*

Other colors: Limelight and limelight frosted.

Reissues: Imperial Glass Company in crystal frosted. Fenton Glass Company (For HCA) in French opalescent, teal blue, and teal blue frosted. Dazell-Viking in pink and pink frosted and again in 1991 in frosted azure blue marked HCA & D, St. Francis DeSales, Newark, Ohio 1842–1992.

Note: Heisey frosted the entire figurine while Imperial at first frosted all but the face. Later Imperial marked theirs IG & LIG. In 1979 Imperial started frosting the entire figurine, including the face; however, they are marked IG. The figurines in limelight are very rare and expensive.

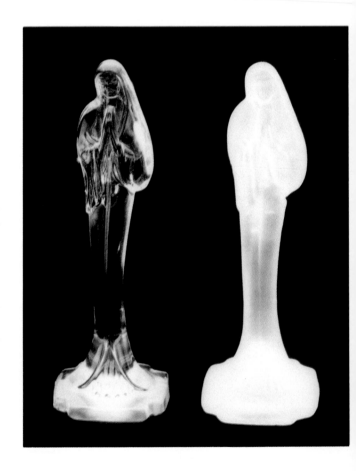

Mike Owens Bust. *Crystal frosted, 4½" high, 5⅛" long (base), 1923. Not marked. $35.00–55.00.*

Other colors: Moongleam and possibly flamingo.

Reissues: None.

Note: Mike Owens invented machinery which automated the production of glass in the early 1900's. His first machine was made specifically for bottles but was later expanded into other phases of glass making. Mike Owens was a partner at the time of his death in 1923, with Edward Drummond Libbey, in the Libbey-Owens Glass Company. Edward Libbey commissioned Heisey Glass Company to produce the bust of Mike Owens in 1923. It is hollow and the quality of glass is fair to good. Across the bottom of the front is embossed, "1859 M.J. Owens 1923."

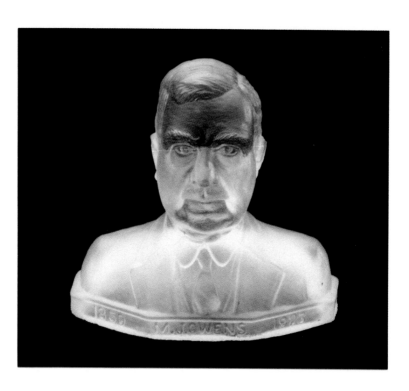

Toy Horse Head Bookend. *3½" high, 3" long from tip of nose to back of base.*

1984	*Crystal, $40.00–60.00.*	
1984	*Crystal Frosted**	
1985	*Cobalt**	
1986	*Ruby**	
1987	*Light Blue**	

*Available in frosted at H.C.A. Museum at $35.00 each.

This item is not from a Heisey mold. In 1984, Heisey Collectors of America Inc. had the mold made with intentions of selling them as a fund raiser. After the mold was made, Viking Glass Company made the horse heads. The figurine is scaled down from the Horse Head Bookend introduced in 1939. (See page 97.) Those produced in 1984 have a ⅞" diameter x ⅛" deep indentation on the very bottom which bears the mark "1984." Thereafter they were marked HCA and the year.

Imperial Glass Company
Bellaire, Ohio

Large Swan. *(Left). Caramel slag, 8" long, 1969. $70.00–80.00.*
Small Swan. *(Right). Caramel slag, 4" high, 1970. $35.00–45.00.*

Other colors: Large Swan: Purple slag, glossy, 1969–75; purple slag, satin, 1973–75; caramel slag, glossy, 1969–76; caramel slag satin, 1973–76; jade slag, 1975–76. Small swan: Steigel green, ritz blue, amber, rose pink, Imperial green, and milk glass (many iridized with a carnival-type finish); purple and jade slags, glossy or satin finish.

Later colors: Large Swan: Horizon blue, pink and meadow green iridized (sold through Levay Distributors under "Imperial By Lenox".)

Note: Large swan reissued in 1990 in crystal for sale in Fostoria's outlet stores.

Imperial Glass Company, one of this country's best-known glass houses, was organized in 1901 by a group of prominent citizens of Wheeling, West Virginia, just across the Ohio River from Bellaire. Production started in January of 1904.

During the Depression Years, 1931 saw Imperial in bankruptcy, being allowed to continue operations during the proceedings. Reorganization followed, and the Imperial Glass Corporation continued uninterrupted production until 1984.

An overall picture of Imperial Glass Company with regard to their glass animal production would include

the "black suede" eagle items; the famous four parlor pups; eagle candle adapter; swans and beautiful slag animals, as well as the prestigious Cathay Crystal line.

In 1964, Imperial produced an Elegant Eagle in crystal (same as Cambridge Eagle shown on page 9.) Production was discontinued in 1968. Note to collectors: if purchased before 1964, the eagle would be Cambridge.

Imperial made many reissues of Heisey animals in crystal between 1964 and 1967, and again in the later years in both crystal and color. See pages 125–139 for that production.

Hootless Owl. *Caramel slag, 4" high, 1969–77. $40.00–50.00.*
Marmota Sentinel (Woodchuck). *Caramel slag, 4½" high, 1969–76. $50.00–60.00.*

Other colors: Crystal (original issue). Woodchuck also came in amber.

Reissues: Both reissued in 1983 for Mirror Images in ultra blue.

Note: Boyd Glass owns the Marmota Sentinel mold as of 1985 and bears the Boyd logo.

#4 "Terrier" Pup. *Amethyst carnival, 3½" high, circa 1980. $35.00–45.00. (The amethyst carnival color was in production for approximately four months.)*
#2 "Scottie-Type" Pup, Standing. *Amber, 2½" high. (Commemorative issue, dated 1983 in raised numbers, and the initials: NIGCS around the tail.)*

Reissues: Reissued in 1983 for Mirror Images, ultra blue, all four pups.

Note: Boyd Art Glass has owned all four Parlor Pup molds since 1985, and they now bear the Boyd logo.

Left to right:

#1 "Bulldog-Type" Pup. *Milk glass, glossy, 3½" high. $45.00–65.00.*
#3 Pup with Tongue Out. *Doeskin*, 3½" high. $55.00–65.00.*
#1 "Bulldog-Type" Pup. *Doeskin*, 3½" high. $55.00–65.00.*

*Doeskin is Imperial's bisque-like matte finished milk glass (frosted milk glass would be a familiar phrase), was introduced in 1952.

Other colors: Milk glass, original issue, circa 1952. Doeskin, 1953. Caramel slag, #1, 1969–76, #2, 1969–70, #3, 1969–70, #4, 1969–76. Amethyst carnival, 1981 (only #4 and #1 pups made). Amber commemorative, 1983. Crystal, all four pups, circa 1965.

Reissues: Mirror Images, in ultra blue, 1983.

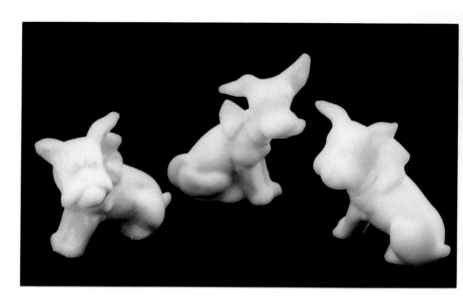

Federal Column Bookends. *(Old style). Crystal, 9" tall, (note oval medallion on center column), accompanied by "Candlewick" eagle adapter with peg bottom and natural back, 5½" tall, crystal. Rarity prohibits pricing.*

Note: These Federal Column Bookends are more often seen in the 4½" height, with the medallion removed and a star at the top of each of the seven columns. Crystal set (including eagle adapters), $350.00–450.00.
 The "Candlewick" eagle adapter is also made with a candle well, behind the eagle, for use with flower frogs and candleholders.
 The 4½" bookends also came in black suede, plain, or with gold trim. The eagle adapter also came in a lalique-like (frosted) and/or bright gold finish. See black suede reprint, page 121.

#1776/3 "Candlewick" Eagle Mirror. *Black milk glass, 6½" high, 1942–50. Rare. $200.00–250.00.*

Other colors: Crystal, crystal with bright gold trim, frosted crystal, and antique blue.

Early 1950's "Black Suede" line!

Note: Beginning price for eagle bookends would be $1,300.00–1,400.00.

Two-Piece Owl Jar. *Caramel slag, with glass eyes, 6½" high, original issue. $55.00–65.00.*
Two-Piece Owl Jar. *Horizon blue carnival, with glass eyes, 6½" high, later issue. $35.00–45.00.*

Other original colors: Purple and jade slag, glossy or satin finish, mid 1970's, will command a higher price. Milk glass and doeskin (frosted milk glass).

Later colors: Pink and meadow green iridized.

Note: Summit Art Glass now owns this mold, as well as the owl creamer and sugar.

Imperial Cathay Crystal
Bellaire, Ohio

Egrette. Cranberry satin, 9½" high, (later issue), 1964–66. $125.00–175.00.
Egrette. Crystal and satin combination, original issue, marked "Virginia B. Evans," 1949. $275.00–300.00.

Note: Reissued by Imperial in verde green satin, 1964–66; crystal, 1964–68.

Cathay Crystal was conceived and designed by Virginia B. Evans in 1949. ("Cathay" is the name given to China by Marco Polo.) Representative of China's history, this line consisted of 38 designs, which were produced in a crystal/satin frosted combination. Except for items too small to accommodate it, each piece bears the script signature of its designer.

The line was lavishly introduced at the National China & Glass Show in Pittsburgh in 1949. Items from the Cathay line were presented in boxes lined with green suede and lettered in gold – each piece having its own number.

But, as was often true for unusual art glass lines, Cathay Crystal did not meet sales expectations, and the line was manufactured for only two years. Sales halted in 1957 when the supply was depleted. Short supply and high demand have made this a very desirable collectible.

Later, for a short time, and in limited production, some designs were produced in color, but the Evans name was removed from the molds. The phoenix bowl appeared in black suede during the 1980's, marked "A.L.I.G." In 1981, several Cathay designs appeared in the Imperial-Lenox Catalog in dark jade green.

Virginia B. Evans passed away in 1983 at the age of 89.

The following four photos depict animal production from the Cathay Crystal line.

Phoenix Bowl. *Dynasty jade (later issue), 5"high, 1960–61. $150.00–175.00.*
Phoenix Bowl. *Crystal and satin combination, original issue, marked: "Virginia B. Evans." $300.00–350.00.*

Reissues: In crystal for sale in Fostoria's outlet stores, 1990.

Note: Reissued by Imperial:

1964–66	Cranberry satin and verde green satin
1954–55	Black Suede
1981	Dark jade
1980's	Black Suede, marked "ALIG"

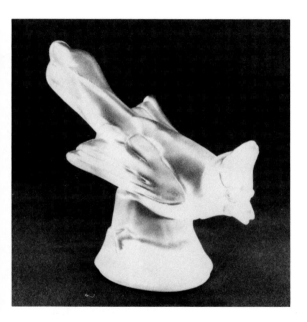

Scolding Bird. *Crystal and satin combination, 5" high, 1949, original issue, signed: "Virginia B. Evans." $150.00–175.00.*

Note: Reissued by Imperial in 1964–68 and called "Nosy Jaybird," also made in black suede. Reissued by Imperial in 1982–83 in caramel slag, marked "ALIG" (glossy finish only).

Dragon Candleholder. *Crystal and frosted combination, 1949. Original issue signed "Virginia B. Evans." Pair, 350.00–400.00.*

Cambridge By Imperial

Scottie Dog Bookend. *Caramel slag, 6½" high, 1982–83. Marked "ALIG," (made over Cambridge mold). Each, $85.00–100.00.*

"Draped Lady." *Made for Mirror Images, 1985. Ruby sunset, 8½" high, marked "IG." Note ribbed base with holes. $45.00–55.00.*

Other colors: Cobalt, vaseline (plain, iridized, or frosted).

"Venus Rising." *Made for Mirror Images, 1981. Ruby sunset, 6½" high, on ribbed base, without holes, marked "IG–81." $20.00–30.00.*

Note: Both are old Cambridge Glass Company molds.

"Venus Rising." *Made for Mirror Images, 1981. Caramel slag, 6½" high, on solid ribbed base, signed "IG–81." Also made in matte caramel slag. $65.00–75.00.*

Other colors: Midnight magic, ruby sunset, pink pixie, green goddess, forever amber, blue belle (plain, frosted, or carnival in all colors.)

Imperial Logo. *Found in cobalt and crystal.*
Clydesdale. *Ultra blue, 5¼" high, 1984, for Mirror Images – ALIG. $95.00–125.00.*

Other colors, Mid 1980's, all marked ALIG: Amber, $300.00–325.00; antique blue, $325.00–350.00; verde green, $125.00–150.00; rose pink, $425.00–450.00; salmon, $300.00–325.00; frosted crystal, feasibility item. (Amber, verde green, and ultra blue came plain or frosted.)

Note: The clydesdale in antique blue had a blistery, bubbly effect covering the entire area – none were sold to customers.

Volumes have been written about Imperial, therefore, it is almost impossible to condense their animal production into one chapter! We feel, however, the following photos and information will afford an in-depth look at this company's Heisey by Imperial animal production.

It is a well known fact in the collecting field that after the A.H. Heisey Company closed in 1957, Imperial Glass Company bought the existing molds. Imperial produced a number of animals in crystal, between 1964 and 1967, and again in the later years, in both crystal and color, before the closing in 1984. For their crystal production see page 139.

A question most often asked by collectors is: "How do you tell the difference in crystal animals produced by Imperial from those produced by Heisey?" The late Clarence Vogel, a pioneer in literature on Heisey, was a firm believer that a black light would show the difference between the two. Mr. Vogel's theory contends that under a black light, Heisey animals will have yellow tones, while those made by Imperial will reflect only the color of the light. Experiments have been done using this method and found it to be true on the items tested. For the complete story on the Heisey molds, refer to that chapter.

Various trademarks were used during Imperial's early production. Approximately 1951 to 1973, Imperial's trademark would be an I and G superimposed. The "I" has curved ends and a dot at the top:

In 1973, Lenox bought Imperial and the trademark changed to "L.I.G." In 1981, Arthur R. Lorch became the owner of Imperial and the trademark became "A.L.I.G."

Mr. Stahl became the final owner of Imperial Glass, when it was down to just 14 employees. During this final period of time, Imperial struggled to stay open. To meet payroll and "keep the wolf away from the door," some animals were made in various colors, but just a <u>few of each.</u> This production may bear the trademark "N.I." (new Imperial).

A great deal of the information contained in this chapter, with regard to color, numbers produced, and fair market value, was compiled through actual auction sheets, closing inventory sheets, Imperial Hayshed, and many years of experience in the marketplace.

In most cases, frosted issues of animals tend to bring a lower price. But, we have noticed in recent auctions that some of the frosted issue brought higher prices than the clear issue.

The following pages refer to "horizon blue" as being a light blue, while "cobalt" is referred to as ultra blue. In the late 1970's, Imperial made a special pour, referred to as "Fortney," of the three ponies: kicking, standing, and balking. These may be seen on page 127.

In 1981, Imperial made special items for Mirror Images and they can be seen on pages 126, 127, 129, 130, and 134.

Feasibility items are not priced as they were extremely limited in production.

Throughout this chapter, we have tried to use Imperial's designated names for their production of the Heisey animal molds.

All inquiries will be answered by the authors. Please include a self-addressed, stamped envelope.

Scottie Champ. *Ultra blue clear, 3½" high, 1982. Made for Mirror Images, ALIG. $55.00–65.00. 1964–67 original issue was crystal.*

Other colors: 1969–70, caramel slag, $125.00–150.00. 1978, milk glass for HCA (Heisey Collectors of America), $45.00–55.00. Mid 1980's, amber, $225.00–250.00; sunshine yellow, $225.00–250.00; nut brown, $75.00–100.00; black, $125.00–150.00; horizon blue, feasibility item. Both amber and ultra blue came in clear and/ or frosted.

Champ Terrier. *Ultra blue clear, 5¾" high, 1982. Made for Mirror Images, ALIG. $75.00–85.00. 1964–67 original issue was crystal.*

Other colors: 1969–73, caramel slag, $100.00–125.00. Black, feasibility item. Both amber and ultra blue came in clear and/or frosted.

Mother Pig. *Ultra blue, 3⅛" high, 1983. Made for Mirror Images, ALIG. $90.00–100.00.*

Other colors: Mid 1980's: crystal, $250.00–275.00; pink, $225.00–250.00; black, $175.00–200.00; amber, $400.00–425.00; ruby, $200.00–225.00; salmon/pink, $275.00–300.00.

Note: Amber and ultra blue issue of Mother Pig came in plain or frosted.

Standing Piglet. *Ultra blue, ⅞" high, 1983. Made for Mirror Images, ALIG. $35.00–45.00.*

Other colors: Mid 1980's: crystal, $30.00–50.00, ruby, $85.00–95.00; crystal, $20.00–25.00; amber, $65.00–75.00; ultra blue (iridized or frosted), $35.00–45.00.

Note: Sitting Piglet, 1" high, not shown here. Colors: Ruby, $85.00–95.00; crystal, $20.00–25.00; amber, $65.00–75.00.

"3 Sons." *Made for Dan Fortney, 1976. Kicking, ultra blue, 4⅛" high, $30.00–50.00. Standing, ultra blue, 5" high, $55.00–75.00. Balking, ultra blue, 3¾" high, $25.00–45.00. (Original 1964–67 issue was crystal.) The following gives the approximate numbers made in 1976 for special order: standing, 1,000; kicking, 1,500; balking, 1,500.*

Note: Many people refer to Imperial's "ultra blue" as "cobalt," but there is little resemblance to Heisey's cobalt when they are seen together. The above colts are marked "IG" and are not ordinarily polished on the bottom.

"3 Sons." *Ruby issue by Dalzell-Viking, marked, circa 1990. Balking, ruby, 3¾" high, $95.00–125.00. Standing, ruby, 5"high, $95.00–125.00. Kicking, ruby, 4⅛"high, $95.00–100.00.*

Other colors: All listed below marked IG (made by Imperial).

1969–78, caramel slag, standing, $35.00–45.00
balking, $140.00–150.00
kicking, $170.00–180.00

1984, amber, standing, $90.00–140.00
balking, $90.00–140.00
kicking, $90.00–140.00

1979, horizon blue, standing, $30.00–35.00
balking, $30.00–35.00
kicking, $30.00–35.00

1979, aqua blue, standing, $65.00–85.00
balking, $65.00–85.00
kicking, $65.00–85.00

1976, ultra blue, Fortney, see page 127.

1984, sunshine yellow (for HCA), standing, $25.00–45.00
balking, $25.00–45.00
kicking, $25.00–45.00

Note: Both amber and sunshine yellow came in plain or frosted. Standing pony in milk glass and black opaque (feasibility items).

Gazelle. *Ultra blue clear, 11" high, 1982. Made for Mirror Images, marked: ALIG. $100.00–125.00. Also made in ultra blue frosted.*

Other colors: Black (very few), $375.00–400.00; crystal, 1982, marked A.L.I.G., $300.00–350.00.

Note: Earlier ultra blue issue marked with Diamond H. Heisey did not make this gazelle in cobalt!

Fish Candlestick. *Sunshine yellow, clear, 5" high, 1982, for HCA, IG. $35.00–45.00.*
Fish Match Holder. *Sunshine yellow, clear, 3" high, 1982, for HCA, IG. $15.00–20.00.*

Note: Also came in sunshine yellow frosted.

Sittin' Duck. *Nut brown, 4½" high, 1983, marked IG. $100.00–110.00.*
Duckling, Floating. *Ultra blue, 2½" high, 1983, made for Mirror Images, IG. $35.00–45.00.*
Duckling, Standing. *Sunshine yellow, 2⅝" high, 1983, made for HCA, IG. $20.00–25.00.*

Other colors: Sitting Duck, 1969–78 caramel slag, $35.00–45.00; 1982 milk glass, $65.00–75.00; 1984 pink, $200.00–225.00; 1982 sunshine yellow (for HCA), $40.00–45.00; 1983 ultra blue (for Mirror Images), $40.00– 45.00. Standing Duckling, 1983 ultra blue (for Mirror Images), $35.00–45.00. Floating Duckling, 1981 sunshine yellow (for HCA), $20.00–25.00.

Note: 1964–67 Sittin' Duck original issue was crystal. Both ultra blue and sunshine yellow came in plain and/or frosted. Both ducklings were reissued in ruby by Dalzell-Viking, 1991, marked D & HCA.

Filly #1, Head Forward. *Crystal frosted, 8½" high, 1982, ALIG. $65.00– 75.00.*
Filly #1, Head Forward. *Amber, 8½" high, 1982, ALIG. $175.00–200.00.*

Other colors: Black (9 made), $400.00– 425.00; salmon/pink, $240.00–265.00; crystal, $125.00–150.00. All marked ALIG.

Note: In 1982 a limited edition of 1,000 head forward Filly was issued, marked ALIG. This issue was accompanied by a certificate of authority, and numbered. $125.00– 150.00. See page 138 for listing of Filly #2, head back.

Wings Down. *Horizon blue, 4½" high, 1980, made for HCA, IG.*
Wings Up. *Horizon blue, 6¾" high, 1980, made for HCA, IG.*
Wings Half. *Horizon blue, 5" high, 1980, made for HCA, IG. Set, $65.00–75.00.*

Other colors: 1964–67 original issue was crystal. All three also made in horizon blue frosted. 1969–78 caramel slag (all three), see page 134. 1984 amber (all three), plain or frosted, set $400.00–425.00. Wings Down in black opaque, feasibility item. Wings Up in milk glass, feasibility item.

Note: Reissued for HCA (all three) in ruby by Dalzell-Viking (200 sets), marked D & HCA, 1990.

Mallards Three.

Small Elephant. *Pink satin, 4½" high, 1980, LIG. $65.00–70.00.*

Other colors: (early to mid 1980's): crystal, $150.00–175.00; meadow green, $110.00–120.00; pink, plain or iridized, $65.00–70.00; milk glass, $125.00–135.00; horizon blue, $175.00–200.00; nut brown, $110.00–120.00; caramel slag, $65.00–85.00; salmon/pink, $200.00–225.00; charcoal, feasibility item.

Note: Charcoal, horizon blue, milk glass, and nut brown came in plain and/or frosted. Reissued by Fenton in French opalescent with hand-painted flowers, 1988. Reissued in 1992 by Fenton in sea mist green, plain or frosted, for HCA.

Medium Eminent Elephant.
*Meadow green carnival, 4" high.
$85.00–95.00.*
Wild Jack. *Meadow green carnival,
6½" high. $85.00–95.00.*

*Note: Both of these animals were
made in 1980 in a limited edition
of 750 sets, marked LIG, and numbered – for Imperial customers and
dealers.*

Imperial Logo. *Crystal.*
Hen. *Charcoal satin, 4½" high, 1980, feasibility item, marked IG.*

Note: See page 136 for further issue of this hen.

Mother Rabbit. *Milk glass, 4⅝"high, 1978, made for HCA, IG. $45.00–50.00.*
Baby Rabbit, Head Up. *Milk glass, 2⅜" high, 1977, made for HCA, IG. $20.00–25.00.*
Baby Rabbit, Head Down. *Milk glass, 2⅜"high, 1977, made for HCA, IG. $20.00–25.00.*

Other colors: Mother, 1982 caramel slag, $250.00–275.00; verde green, $225.00–250.00; ultra blue, $150.00–175.00; sunshine yellow, $225.00–250.00. All marked IG. Bunnies, head up, 1982, ultra blue, $45.00–55.00; head down, 1982, ultra blue, $45.00–55.00; sunshine yellow, $70.00–80.00.

Reissues: Bunny, head down, 1982–83, caramel slag, marked ALIG, $45.00–55.00. Both bunnies reissued in 1990 by Dalzell-Viking, ruby, marked HCA. Both bunnies reissued in 1991 by Dalzell-Viking, pink, plain or frosted, marked HCA.

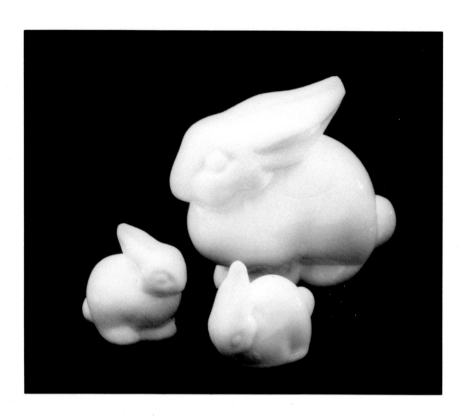

Cygnet. *Ruby, 2½" high, made by Dalzell-Viking, marked D & HCA. $20.00–25.00.*
Cygnet. *Black, 2½" high, 1984, ALIG. $45.00–55.00.*

Other colors: 1980 – horizon blue, plain or frosted (for HCA), $20.00–25.00; milk glass and pink satin (feasibility item). 1982–83 – caramel slag, marked ALIG, $40.00–45.00.

Angelfish Bookend. *Ruby (also made in ruby frosted), 6⅝" high, 1984. $300.00–325.00.*

Other colors: 1984, amber, plain or frosted, $125.00–150.00; horizon blue, $125.00–150.00; sunshine yellow, $175.00–200.00; verde green, $100.00–110.00.

Note: The above listed colors were made in very limited editions during Imperial's last year.

The following listed animals, <u>not pictured previously</u> in the chapter, were made in various colors (and some crystal) by Imperial using Heisey molds, during the early to mid 1980's, before Imperial's closing in 1984. Keep in mind that production was <u>very limited!</u> See pages 125 and 126 for trademark information.

Imperial Name:	Colors:
Angry Cockerel, 8" high (Fighting Rooster)	Pink, plain and/or carnival
Asiatic Pheasant, 10½" high	Amber, crystal
Caballo Pegasso, 8⅞" high (Flying Mare)	Amber, sunshine yellow
Elephant, large, 5¼" high	Ultra blue (feasibility item)
El Tauro, 4" high (Bull)	Sunshine yellow, green, nut brown, ultra blue, black, antique blue
Filly #2 (Head Backward)	Amber, crystal, verde green (plain or frosted)
Giraffe, 11" high	Amber (plain or frosted), sunshine yellow, black (feasibility item)
Goose, wings half, 4½" high	Ultra blue
Horsehead Bookend, 6⅞" high	Pink (plain or iridized)
Rearing Horse Bookend, 7⅞" high	Black (plain or frosted)
Regal Ringneck, 4¾" high	Amber, blue iridized, amethyst carnival (feasibility item)
Show Horse, 7⅜" high	Amber, crystal
Sparrow, 2¼" high	Verde green (plain or frosted), 1990–91: Ruby and Biscayne blue by Dalzell-Viking
Superb Swan, 7" high	Horizon blue, black (2 or 3 each)
Tropical Fish, 12" high	Amber, crystal (8 to 10)
Kingfisher Flower Frog	Black (21)

The following listed animals, <u>not previously shown</u> in this chapter, made by Imperial using Heisey molds during the period of 1964–67, may be seen in their crystal issue on page 139. None were marked IG, but some will carry the Diamond H trademark, while others will be unmarked.

Imperial Name:

Angry Cockerel (Fighting Rooster), 8" high	Item #4
Caballo Pegasso (Flying Mare), 8⅞" high	Item #15
El Tauro (Bull), 4" high, very few made	Item #13
Goose Duo (wings half, wings up)	Item #7
Proud Puffer (Pouter Pigeon), 6¼" high	Item #3
Regal Ringneck (Pheasant), 4¾" high	item #6
Superb Swan (Large Swan), 7" high, very few made	Item #16

Note: Since it is very difficult to tell these animals from those produced by Heisey, they are bringing the same price as the Heisey issue. Obviously, these animals are being sold as "Heisey."

Left to right:

Oscar. *Black opaque, by Imperial, 1985.*
Oscar. *Clematis alexandrite, by Viking, 1986.*
Oscar. *Crystal opalescent, by Fenton, 1987.*
Oscar. *Opal white, by Fenton, 1988.*

Note: Not shown is antique blue by Imperial, 1985.

Oscar. *Teal blue/green, by Fenton, 1989.*
Oscar. *Roseline, by Fenton, 1990.*
Oscar. *Sapphire blue opalescent, by Fenton, 1991.*

Note: Not shown is 1990 peach by Fenton; 1991 sapphire blue opalescent frosted by Fenton; and 1992 Burmese (shiny) by Fenton.

Indiana Glass
Dunkirk, Indiana

Pouter Pigeon Bookend. *Crystal, 5½" high. (Also seen with "Czechoslovakia" in raised letters on base.) Pair, $30.00–40.00.*
Horsehead Bookend. *Crystal, 6" high, hollow back. Pair, $20.00–30.00.*

Walking Panther. *Blue, 3" high, 7" long. Rare. $200.00–250.00.*
Walking Panther. *Amber, 3½" high, on marble base. Rare. $200.00–250.00.*

Indiana Glass was incorporated in 1907, producing a general line of hand-pressed wares. Their 1926 line included #610 Pyramid, #304 Soda Fountain, and the Tearoom line. Pieces from these lines are eagerly sought after by today's collectors. Colors are pink, green, amber, yellow, and crystal.

The late 1920's saw a combination of both hand-made and machine-made glassware being produced, and continued on through the years.

Now a subsidiary of Lancaster-Colony, Indiana continues to produce a general line of quality glass.

A later color of the 1950's, teal, was seen in their line of Christmas Candy #624.

Horse Head Bookend. *Milk glass, 6" high, hollow back. Pair, $25.00–35.00.*

Two-Piece Elephant Candy Dish. *Pink, 4" high, 1980's. Market price.*

In 1981, this elephant was produced in crystal and filled with red, white, and blue jelly beans for the "Republicans." Other clear colors were also made.

In 1983, Tiara Glass (Div. of Indiana Glass) made the elephant in frosted colors of pink, blue, and mint green. Tiara now owns this mold.

Presently, an almost identical elephant is appearing on the shelves in ruby, pink, and cobalt (obviously imports).

Note: Co-Operative Flint made this elephant in the 1920's and 1930's with a variation of backs. See page 43.

New Martinsville Glass Company
New Martinsville, West Virginia

**#201 Elephant Incense Burner. *Green with painted decorations, 6" high, circa 1940.*
**#198 Elephant Cigarette Holder. *Pink with decoration, 5" high, circa 1940.*

Other colors: Black amethyst.

New Martinsville Glass Company began operations in New Martinsville, West Virginia in 1901, and was destroyed by fire in 1907. After being rebuilt, the company remained in operation continuously. Glass production of New Martinsville Glass Company can be divided into three periods.

Period I	1901-1907	Art & Opaque Glass
Period II	1907–1937	Pattern Glass
Period III	1937–1944	Crystal Ware Era (animals and figurines)

Very few pieces have been seen with NM incised on the glass.

1944 saw a change in management, and New Martinsville Glass Company was renamed Viking Glass Company. (Rainbow Art Glass was their subsidiary.) Brilliant color continued to play a large part in the allure of this company's wares. The Epic Line was born; swans in all color combinations and sizes continued; and flat-sided animals came into the line. Production was usually marked with a paper label designed with a Viking boat.

Viking also made the magnificent ruby animals for Mirror Images. A raised "V" will be found on this series.

In 1986, when Viking Glass Company closed their doors, it seemed to end an era of American handmade glass. However, in 1987, Mr. Kenneth Dalzell (long associated with Fostoria Glass Company) purchased the defunct Viking Glass Company, reopening its doors under the banner of Dalzell-Viking Glass Company.

Many of the old New Martinsville/Viking animals, as well as Barth Art molds were in production again. Made in crystal, frosted crystal, and black, these animals bear the name "Dalzell" acid-etched on the bottom. The "seconds" are marked "DX" and sold in their outlet stores.

New production of the old animals is so noted under their photo.

Basic colors for New Martinsville/Viking lines are crystal, charcoal, ruby, cobalt, ebony, evergreen, emerald green, olive green, amber, amethyst, amberina, persimmon, lime, pink, peach, and milk glass. Frosted colors are midnight (frosted ebony), glamour gold (frosted amber), cherry glo (frosted pink), glamour green (frosted green), grey mist (frosted charcoal), driftwood (brown milk glass) and peach melba (frosted peach).

Note: Items in this chapter preceded by double asterisk (**) are from a private collection and cannot be priced.

#766 Porpoise on Wave. *Crystal, 6" high, also came in clear/frosted combo. Original issue, $400.00–500.00.*

Note: In 1985–86, Viking made a special pour in crystal for Sea World. 1988–90 Dalzell-Viking in crystal and frosted.

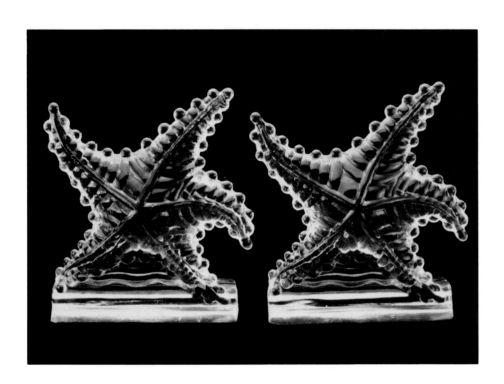

Starfish. *Crystal, 7¾" high. $65.00–85.00 each.*

#452 Seal, Large with Ball. *Crystal, 7" high, 1938–51. $50.00–75.00.*
#452 Seal, Large with Candleholder and "Janice Pattern" Ivy Bowl. *Crystal, 12" high, 1938–51. Seal, $75.00–95.00. Ivy bowl, $25.00–45.00.*
#435 Seal, Baby with Candleholder. *Crystal, 4½" high. $50.00–70.00. Also came with ball on nose.*

Other colors: Large seals: completely frosted, frosted with clear ball, clear with ruby ball, black with ruby ivy bowl. Small seals: frosted. Ivy bowl: emerald green.

Note: Large seal (no ball or candleholder), and small seal with ball reissued by Dalzell-Viking in crystal, 1988–91. In the mid 1980's small seal with ball was reissued for Mirror Images in ruby plain, satin, or carnival (2nd in a series of five), limited edition of 500, made by Viking and marked with a "V" and "MI." *See page 154.*

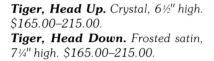

Tiger, Head Up. *Crystal, 6½" high. $165.00–215.00.*
Tiger, Head Down. *Frosted satin, 7¼" high. $165.00–215.00.*

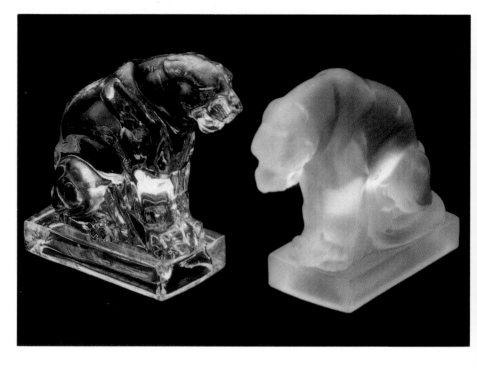

Horse, Head Up. *Crystal, 8" high.*
$75.00–95.00.
Gazelle, Leaping. *Crystal wtih*
frosted base, 8¼" high, (gazelle also
totally frosted). $45.00–65.00.

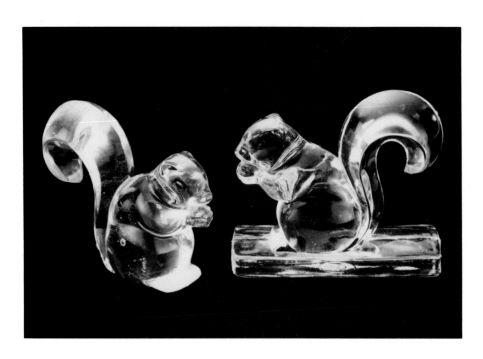

#674 Squirrel. *Crystal, 4½" high, no base, until 1953. $35.00–45.00.*
#670 Squirrel. *Crystal, 5½" high, square base, until 1950. $45.00–65.00.*

Note: Squirrel on square base also reported in light blue and frosted with clear
base.

#716 Wolfhound. *Crystal, 7" high, until 1950. $75.00–95.00.*

Reissues: By Dalzell-Viking, in crystal 1988–90, and in black in 1991.

#733 Police Dog. *(German Shepherd). Crystal, 5" high, 1937–50. Also made as a lamp base in pink. $55.00–75.00.*

Reissues: In 1978 by Viking, with the following appearing on the base: "4/100; the NM incised on side of base; and paper label with Viking emblem." Also reissued in the mid 1980's for Mirror Images in ruby, plain, satin, or carnival by Viking, (3rd in a series of five), limited edition of 500, marked with a "V."

#669, Hen. *Crystal, 5" high, until 1948. $55.00–65.00.*
#668 Rooster with Crooked Tail. *Crystal, 7½" high, until 1951. $65.00–85.00.*
#667 Chick. *Crystal, 1" high, until 1948. $20.00–25.00.*
#667 Chick. *Frosted, 1" high, until 1948. $20.00–25.00.*

Other colors: Chick also came in cobalt, $75.00–95.00; rooster came in frosted.

Reissues: Hen and rooster reissued by Dalzell-Viking in crystal in 1988.

#237 Elephant Bookend. *Crystal, 5½" high, until 1945. $65.00–85.00.*

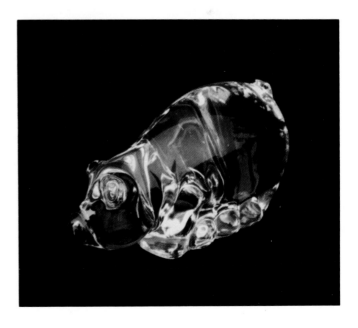

****#1 Design, Mama Pig.** *Crystal, 3" high, 6" long, with nursing piglets attached (three on each side), limited edition.*

Note: As this original design was considered to be in "bad taste," the pig and piglets were separated in Design #2. Approximately 200 were made of Design #1.

#2 Design, #762 Mama Pig. *Crystal, 4" high, 6½" long, until 1953. $250.00–350.00.*
#763 Piglets. *Crystal, 1" high, 2" long, until 1953. $75.00–125.00.*

Other colors: Mama Pig also came in frosted.

Reissues: Mama Pig reissued by Dalzell-Viking in crystal 1990, in black 1991.

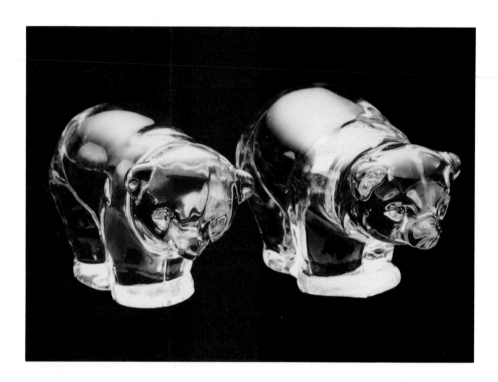

#488 Mama Bear. *Crystal, solid, 4" high, 6" long, 1938–51. $175.00–225.00.*
#489 Papa Bear. *Crystal, solid, 4" high, 6½" long, 1938–51. $200.00–250.00.*

Reissues: In 1985 Mama Bear was made by Viking for Mirror Images, 1st in a series of five, marked with a "V," in ruby plain, satin, or carnival. See page 154. 1988–90 Mama was reissued by Dalzell-Viking in crystal and in black in 1991.

Note: Mama Bear's head is slightly turned, and Papa Bear has little rolls of fat under his chin. There is ½" difference in their length.

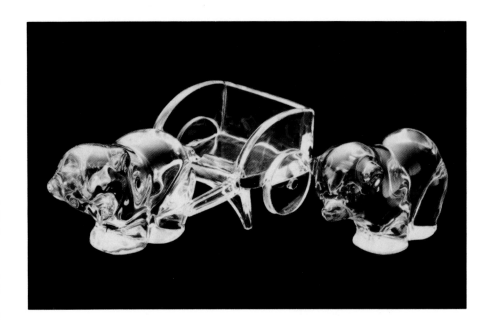

Baby Bear, Head Turned. Crystal, 3" high, until 1954. $40.00–60.00.

#508 Cigarette Cart. Crystal, 5" long, until 1954. $10.00–15.00.

#487 Baby Bear, Head Straight. Crystal, 3" high, until 1954. $40.00–60.00.

Other colors: Baby Bears also came in frosted crystal, few in milk glass. Limited run in black with cart, $200.00–225.00 set.

Reissues: Baby Bear, head straight, reissued for Mirror Images by Viking in mid 1980's, in ruby plain, satin, or carnival, 4th in a series of five, limited edition of 500, marked with a "V." See page 154.

#487 Baby Bear, head straight, reissued by Dalzell-Viking, 1988 crystal, 1990 crystal, and 1990–91 black.

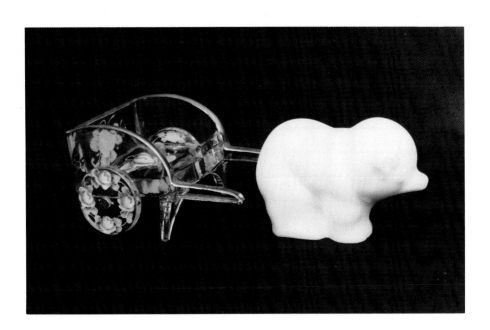

Baby Bear, Head Turned. Milk glass, 3" high, with #508 Cigarette Cart, crystal with Charleton hand-painted flowers, 5" long.

Mama Bear. *Ruby plain, satin, or carnival, 4¾" high, 1985. Made for Mirror Images by Viking, 1st in a series of five, limited edition of 500, marked with a "V." $65.00–85.00.*

#733 Police Dog. *(German Shepherd). Pink, 6" high, oval base, generally used for a lamp base. $70.00–90.00.*

Baby Seal with Ball. *Ruby, 4½" high, mid 1980's. $40.00–60.00.*
Baby Bear, Head Straight. *Ruby, 3" high, mid 1980's. $40.00–60.00.*

Reissues: Made by Viking over New Martinsville molds for Mirror Images, plain, satin, or carnival finish, limited edition of 500 each, marked with a "V."

#764 Large Mama Rabbit. *Crystal, 2½" high, until 1945. $250.00–350.00.*
Bunny, Head Up, Ears Back. *Amber, 1" high. $40.00–60.00.*
Bunny, Ears Up. *Amber, 1" high. $40.00–60.00.*

Other colors: Bunnies were made in crystal. Cobalt and red, $65.00–75.00 each.

Reissues: Reissued in 1986 by Viking for Mirror Images in ruby plain, satin or carnival, 5th in a series of five, limited edition of 500, marked with a "V." Mama Rabbit was reissued by Dalzell-Viking in 1988–90 in crystal and frosted, and in black in 1990.

**#761 Pelican with Elongated Neck.
Pink, 11" high. One of a kind.

#761 Pelican. *Crystal. 8" high, until 1945. $75.00–95.00.*

Reissues: In crystal by Dalzell-Viking, 1990.

#509 Eagle. *Crystal, 8" high, circa 1938. $65.00–75.00.*

Reissues: In crystal and frosted by Dalzell-Viking, 1988, 1990, and 1991.

**Carriage Horse Bookend. *Pink, 7½" high, 1940's.*

Other colors: Crystal and peach satin.

Note: See comparison sheet of Rearing Horses, page 231.

#497 Hunter/Woodsman. *Crystal, 7⅜" high, on square base. $75.00–95.00.*

Note: Also came on round base.

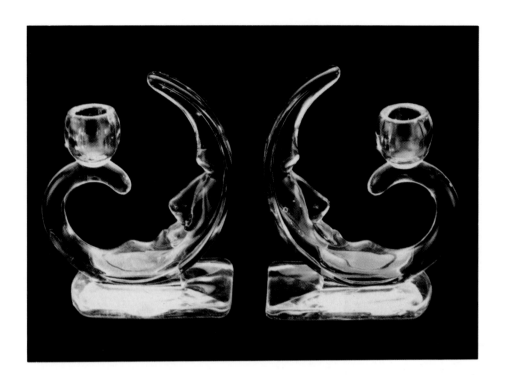

Man-In-The-Moon Candlesticks.
Crystal, 6½" high. Very unusual and scarce. Pair, $200.00–225.00.

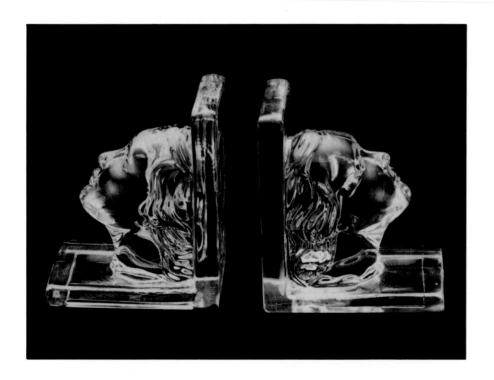

Lady Face Bookends. *Crystal, 5¼". Rare. Pair, $195.00–200.00.*

Note: Also seen marked "Czechoslovakia" on back of base at bottom (base being slightly different in design).

Nautilus Bookend. *Crystal, 6" high. $25.00–35.00.*

Other colors: Frosted crystal.

#499 Clipper Ship Bookends. *Crystal, 5¾" high, 1938. Pair, $75.00–95.00.*

Note: Similar bookends were made by U.S. Glass Company, circa 1925, in black or amber satin.

Dancing Lady Flower Frog. *Pink satin, 6¼" high, 1940's. $400.00–450.00.*

Other colors: Crystal frosted.

**#1926 Nice Kitty Good Night Set. *Green with painted decorations, 1926. Short pint container with inverted drinking glass.*

Other colors: Crystal, black, amber, blue, green, and rose, plain or frosted.

Note: Similar decanter made by Cambridge.

**#1926 Volstead Pup Decanter. *Crystal with painted decoration, 10½"high, 1926.*

Other colors: Full range of colors, all decorated.

Note: This pup holds a pint! His hat is a tumbler. A similar decanter was made by Cambridge.

The Janice Line of tableware, itself, was introduced in 1926. In 1930, to induce higher sales, crystal necks and heads were applied to this line, and it became known as "Swan Janice S-Line." See page 162.

Colored necks and heads were forthcoming in the early 1940's, (see page 162), as well as colored bodies with crystal necks and heads (see page 163).

Production of this line, in many different combinations of crystal and color, as well as hand-decorated, silver overlay, and gold decorated, continued into the 1970's. Some production had small collar bases on the bowls, whereas others had ground and polished bottoms.

The following listings are representative of the Swan "Janice" S-Line:

#4543	1SJ	Single Swan, bowl, small, tail pulled down for spout
#412	2SJ	Double Swan, bowl, small
#4528	2SJ	Double Swan, sandwich plate, large
#456	SJ	Double Swan, sugar bowl
	(set)	Single Swan, creamer
#4551	2SJ	Double Swan, bowl, large oval with base
#412	1SJ	Single Swan, ashtray, small
#4565	2SJ	Double Swan, bowl, large round
#4521	1SJ	Single Swan, bowl, long oval
#4521	2SJ	Double Swan, bowl, long oval
#4541	1CSJ	Single Swan, dish, medium, sides pulled in
#443	1SJ	Single Swan, dish, small
#4541	1HSJ	Single Swan, bowl, medium tail pulled down
#4541	1SJ	Single Swan, covered candy dish
#4551	1SJ	Single Swan, bowl, large, tail pulled down

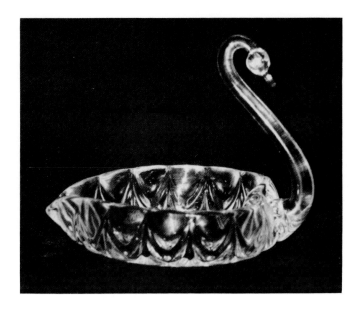

#4541 Bowl, Swan Janice S-Line. *All crystal, 6½" long, ground and polished bottom, 1930–70. $15.00–20.00.*

#4541 Ashtray/Bowl, Swan Janice S-Line. *Crystal with cobalt head and neck, 6½" long, ground and polished bottom, 1940–70. $25.00–30.00.*

#4551 Bowl, Swan Janice S-Line. *Crystal with cobalt head and neck, 9½" long, with collar bottom, 1930–70. $45.00–55.00.*

#4543 Bowl, Swan Janice S-Line. *Ruby with crystal neck, bowl 4¼" high, ground and polished bottom, 1940–70. $50.00–75.00.*

Swans – "S" Line, Plain. 1930's in crystal, 1940's in color.

S-Line double swan handled designs, some plain, some etched (see page 164), would include the following listed pieces:

#137	2SJ	Double Swan, bowl
#237	2SJ	Double Swan, vase
#4550	2SJ	Double Swan, vase, paneled
#111	2SJ	Double Swan, vase, round
#137	2SJ	Double Swan, vase, square
(No number)		Double Swan, perfume bottle, tall (plain or etched)

Swan lines other than Janice S-Line were in production for New Martinsville/Viking during the years of 1940–60. With other Depression Era glass companies manufacturing swans, in all colors and sizes, it is important to know this clue: the necks of the New Martinsville/ Viking swans set into a "V" scallop, directly even with the edge of the dish. Also, the 5" swans, referred to as "sweetheart" shape, have a round collar base. For examples, see pages 164 and 165.

Double Swan-Handled Bowl, S-Line Plain. *Crystal, 1930's. $45.00–55.00.*

#974 Swans. *"Sweetheart" shape, 5", collar bases, 1940–60. Light blue with crystal, $15.00–20.00; ruby candleholder with crystal, $25.00–30.00; ebony with crystal, $20.00–25.00; amber with crystal, $15.00–20.00.*

#974 Swans. *"Sweetheart shape," 5", collar bases, 1940–60. Cobalt with crystal, $20.00–25.00; ruby with crystal, $20.00–25.00; light green with crystal, $15.00–20.00.*

#974 Swan. *"Sweetheart" shape, crystal wtih gold neck, head and floral decoration, 5", collar base. $25.00–30.00.*

Swan Ashtray. *Ebony body with crystal neck and head, indents in tail for cigarette rest. $20.00–25.00.*

Swan Console Bowl. *Emerald green with crystal neck, 11" long. $20.00–25.00.*
Swan Candleholders. *"Sweetheart" shape, emerald green, 5" long. $15.00–20.00.*

The "long" shape of the swan has a flat body with shallow sides and polished bottom rim. Sizes are 4", 7", 10½", and 12½" ovals. This style swan was made in many color combinations, cobalt, ruby, and ebony bring the highest prices. They were made from 1940–60. See below for shape.

Long Oval Swan Shape. *4", $25.00–35.00; 7", $25.00–35.00; 10½", $40.00–50.00; 12½", $50.00–60.00.*

The Princess swan shape of New Martinsville/Viking, #502, has ½" scalloped base and scalloped top edge of bowl. This pattern came in 4½", 8", and 11" sizes (4½" also came as candleholder). Silver overlay has been noted on pieces of the Princess swan line. See below for shape.

Princess Swan Pattern Shape.

Paden City
Paden City, West Virginia

Pheasants, Head Turned. *Pale blue, 12" long. $150.00–200.00 each.*

Other colors: Crystal, circa 1940.

Note: Often referred to as "Bird of Paradise."

Paden City Glass Manufacturing Company, Paden City, West Virginia (1916–1951), is known as "the color company," having made colored glassware continuously, almost from its inception. From the middle 1920's until 1951 when their doors closed, the following colors were in production: opal, ebony, mulberry, cheriglo, yellow, dark green, crystal, red, amber, primrose, rose, light green, and blue. As blue dominated the animals shown in this chapter, the following information is pertinent:

"Paden City made basically two shades of blue: cobalt and a lighter shade. The cobalt color has remained throughout the years. The color was advertised under various names, but seems to have been called 'royal' more often. Paden City's lighter shade of blue was changed several times, and advertised under different names: 'Copen' and 'Neptune.' Possibly more than one shade of light blue may have been in production at the same time. The lighter shade of blue is most commonly a medium blue with a slight royal tint. Another is a very pale watery hue . . ."

Paden City by Jerry Barnett

Note: The blue issue of the Paden City animals brings a substantially higher price.

When a Paden City figurine is identified as "Barth Art," the following applies: Harry Barth was associated with New Martinsville Glass Company as early as 1918. He became General Manager of the company in the late 1930's. He resigned in the early 1940's to form Barth Art Company, an organization of glass grinders, polishers, and decorative cutters. As different molds were completed to Barth's specifications, they were assigned to Paden City Glass Company (and a few other companies) for the manufacturing process. The glassware was then returned to the Barth Art Company for the finishing work, and sold under that company's label.

In 1952 Mr. Barth sold some animal figurine molds to Viking Glass Company, namely: standing and fighting ducks, angelfish, tall pony, and rabbit. See New Martinsville/Viking Glass Company page for illustrations of these designs.

Research has yet to turn up exact production dates for the animals shown in this chapter.

When Paden City closed in 1951, most of their molds were sold to Canton Glass Company of Marion, Indiana.

167

Pheasant (Chinese). *Darker blue, 13¾"
long, circa 1940. $125.00–175.00.*

Other colors: Crystal, lighter blue.

Rooster (Chanticleer). *Pale blue, 9½" high, circa 1940. $150.00–200.00.*
Rooster (Elegant). *Pale blue, 11" high, circa 1940. $200.00–250.00.*

Other colors: Both roosters also made in crystal and/or frosted.

Goose. *Pale blue, 5" high, circa 1940. Scarce.*
$100.00–125.00.

Other colors: Crystal.

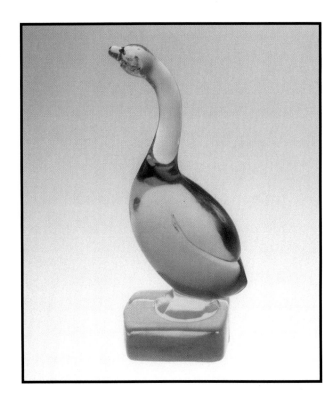

Tall Pony. *Pale blue, 12" high, circa 1940. Barth Art.*
$100.00–150.00.

Other colors: Crystal and crystal/frosted combination;
black will command $300.00–350.00.

Reissues: Made by Viking in 1974, see page 192. Reissued
by Dalzell-Viking in 1990 in crystal, marked "Dalzell" on
bottom.

Tall Pony. *Crystal, 12" high, circa 1940.*
$75.00–95.00.

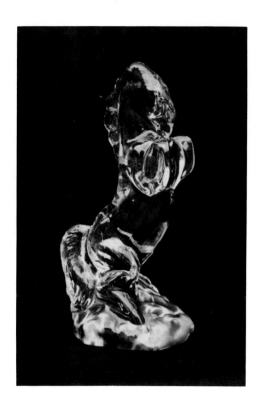

Rearing Horse. *Crystal, 10" high. Barth Art. $150.00–195.00.*

Other colors: Black.

Note: "The Museum of Industrial Arts in Prague, credit this design to Mario Petrucci, an Italian sculptor, produced by a North Bohemian glass factory in the '20s..." (Mary Van Pelt). However, we have only seen this horse with the Barth Art label.

**Pelican. *Crystal, 10" high. Barth Art. Very rare.*

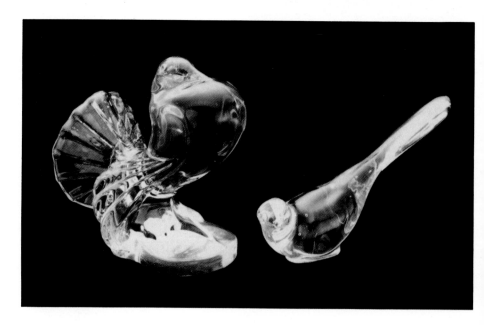

Pouter Pigeon Bookend. *Crystal, 6¼" high. Barth Art. $65.00–85.00.* **Bird.** *Crystal, 5" high (at tip of tail). $25.00–40.00.*

Other colors: Bird also made in light blue.

Note: Original mold for Fenton's Happiness Bird. It is important to explain that Fenton also made the Happiness Bird in light blue. However, Fenton's light blue issue <u>is marked</u>, and Paden City's blue bird <u>is not</u>! It would be hard to tell Paden City's crystal issue from Fenton's early crystal issue as neither was marked. (Fenton's later crystal issue was marked.)

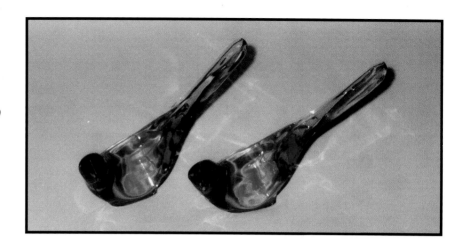

Bird. *Light blue, 5" high. $95.00–125.00 each.*

Rooster, Head Down. *Crystal, 8¾" high. Barth Art. $65.00–85.00.*
Rooster, Barnyard. *Crystal, 8¾" high. $75.00–100.00.*

Other colors: Barnyard rooster also made in darker blue.

Note: Rooster similar to Head Down Rooster made by K.R. Haley and Kemple Glass. See page 87.

Dragon Swans. *Crystal, 9¾" long, slightly hollow bases. $200.00–225.00 each.*

Other colors: Also made in pale blue. Very scarce.

#611 Polar Bear on Ice. *Crystal, 4½" high. $45.00–65.00.*

Reissues: Reissued by Dalzell-Viking in crystal and frosted, 1990–91.

#677 Squirrel on Curved Log. *Crystal, 5½" high. Barth Art. $45.00–65.00.*

Reissues: Reissued by Dalzell-Viking in crystal, 1990–91.

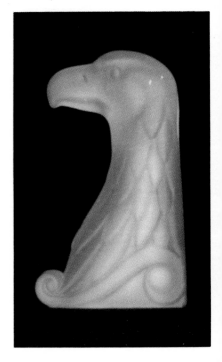

American Eagle Head Bookend. *Crystal frosted, 7½" high. Pair, $250.00–300.00.*

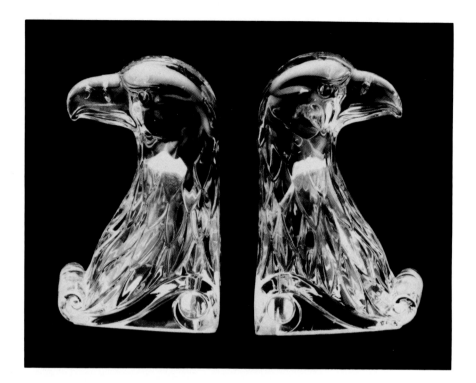

American Eagle Head Bookends.
*Crystal, 7½" high, solid glass with flat back,
weighs 4 lbs. Pair, $250.00–300.00.*

Other colors: Frosted crystal.

Bunny "Cotton Tail" Dispenser, Ears Up. *Frosted blue. $120.00–170.00.*
Bunny "Cotton Tail" Dispenser, Ears Down. *Frosted blue, 5" high. $85.00–95.00.*
Bunny "Cotton Tail" Dispenser, Ears Up. *Frosted blue. $120.00–170.00.*

Other colors: Crystal, pink or blue transparent, frosted pink or crystal, and milk glass.

Note: Ears Up style is hard to find.

L.E. Smith Glass Company
Mt. Pleasant, Pennsylvania

Squirrel. *Frosted satin (crystal was original issue), 4½" high, 1970's. $10.00–15.00.*

Owl on Stump with Rose. *Frosted satin (crystal was original issue), 3½" high, 1960's. $10.00–15.00.*

Lewis E. Smith, a chef in Mt. Pleasant, Pennsylvania, is credited with Smith's early beginnings in 1907, operating from the old deserted Anchor Glass Factory, and making utilitarian glass products. In 1911, Mr. Smith left and the factory changed hands, but retained the L.E. Smith name.

"We're the folks who made the first headlight lens for the Model T Ford, and then went on to invent the non-glare headlights. We also pioneered the famous 'vault lights' – those translucent bricks that allow the light, but not the image, to shine through . . ."

L.E. Smith died in 1931. The plant remained in operation and in 1979 Libbey-Owens Ford became the new owner. This company remains in business today.

Colors produced in the 1920's include green, amber, canary, amethyst, blue, and pink. L.E. Smith is famous for its black glassware, introduced in the late 1920's, some with silver overlay, and some with hand-painted decorations.

The animal line originated in the 1920's with the exception of the owl. Most of the miniatures were also made in larger sizes. They were original designs – none were acquired from other companies. The miniatures were marked with a small "c" in a circle with a small "s" outside the circle, this being Smith's registered trademark.

In addition to the Smith miniatures shown with the Duncan & Miller viking boat, page 57, others would include 1950, 3½" frosted birds, goose girl; and Scottie, large and small. The latter 1960's brought in the cat, owl, and goose (large and small). In 1970, the sparrow, elephant, and frosted squirrel were added. The 1974 catalog shows a new addition of a sitting bear but not the goose, rearing horse, cow, or rabbit. It also shows the bust of the four presidents carved on Mount Rushmore, 6¼" tall (since discontinued).

Most of the L.E. Smith miniatures are being produced today in crystal, frosted satin, some carnivals, and a few ebony.

The 1991 catalog shows these at $8.00–12.00 each:

Small goose, 2½"	Scottie, 2¼" & 3"
Squirrel, 2½"	Mouse, 2"
Owl, 2¼"	Cat, 1¾" & 3"
Rooster, 2¼"	Swan, 4½"
Elephant, 1¾"	Feeding Bird, 3"
Unicorn, 2½"	Standing Bird, 3"
Flying Bird, 9"	

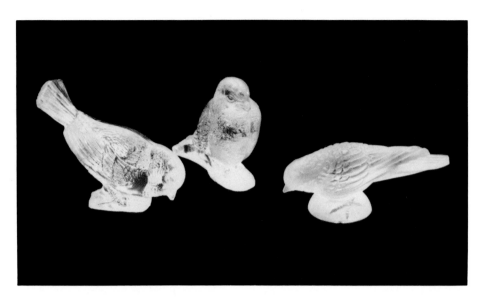

Sparrow, Head Down. *Crystal, 3½"
high, 1950's. $10.00–15.00.*
Sparrow, Head Up. *Crystal, 3½" high,
1950's. $10.00–15.00.*

*Other colors: Both sparrows came in
satin crystal.*

*Note: Lalique Sparrow shown on
right for comparison.*

Camel Lying Down. *Crystal, 4½" high, 6" long, raised Shriners emblem on
neck, raised, square hollow base. $40.00–60.00.*

Other colors: Amber.

*Note: Originally made by Levay Distributors from an old Smith mold.
Smith has recently retrieved this mold.*

Queen Fish Aquarium. *Crystal, 7¼" high, 15" long, mid 1920's. $175.00–225.00.*

Other colors: Green.

Note: Queen Fish aquarium has ribbed body.

King Fish Aquarium. *Green, 7¼" high, 15" long, footed, mid 1920's. $225.00–300.00.*

Other colors: Crystal.

Note: This aquarium also came with a high base, 10" high, 15" long, in green or crystal.

Horse, Lying Down. *Green, 9" long, hollow, 1968. Scarce. $95.00–125.00.*

Other colors: Amber, blue, and amberina.

Note: Made for a short period of time.

Scottie Creamer or Pipe Rest. *Fired-on black (original issue in crystal), 5½" long. $5.00–10.00.*
Duck Ashtray. *Black glass (original issue in crystal), 6½" long. $5.00–10.00.*

Other colors: Scarce green reported for Scottie.

Note: Ashtray is part of a three-piece set: two ashtrays and two-piece Mother Duck cigarette box.

Courtesy Hazel Marie Weatherman

#3/10 Large Swan. Milk glass with decoration, 8½" high, circa 1930's. $25.00–45.00.
#15/10 Small Swan. Milk glass with decoration, 4" high, circa 1930's. $15.00–25.00.

Other colors: Crystal (original issue), crystal frosted, pink, green plain or frosted, and black.

Note: Small swans were also sold through Levay Distributing in carnival colors.

#3/4 Large Swan. Black amethyst with silver trim, 8½" long, 1930's. $25.00–30.00.

Other colors: Smith colors, plain or frosted, some with decoration.

Fighting Cock. Amberina, 9" tall, 1960's. $35.00–45.00.

Other colors: Blue, green, amber, and amberina.

Fighting Cock. *Butterscotch base slag (browns to red swirls), 9" high, 1960's, only 200 pair made. $75.00–100.00 each.*

Rearing Horse Bookend. *Emerald green, 8" high. $25.00–55.00.*

Other colors: 1940's original issue crystal or crystal frosted. Later colors were amberina, blue, amber, and black.

Note: Notice the beaded mane. See page 231 for Rearing Horse Comparison.

Rearing Horse Bookend. *Ebony, 8" high. $45.00–65.00.*

Turkey Two-Piece Candy Dish. *Crystal, 7¼" high. $25.00–45.00.*

Other colors: 1973–74 gold, amber, amethyst, ruby carnival, crystal lustre, green carnival, amberina; 1975–76 amber; 1980 crystal, amberina; 1981 peach lustre; 1982 crystal and crystal frosted with red hand-painted head (made for Levay Glass Company).

Note: Also seen in frosted crystal with ruby flashed tail, wings, and head.

"A glass version of Hummel Figurine #47."

Goose Girl. *Original issue crystal, 6" high, 1950's. $15.00–25.00.*
Goose Girl. *Original issue crystal, 8" high, 1950's. $25.00–45.00.*
Goose Girl. *Satin crystal, later issue, 6" high, 1950's. $15.00–25.00.*

Other colors: Later colors, 1970's, both sizes: amber, green, blue, and flame.

Note: 6" figure was also sold later through Levay Distributors in carnival colors.

Flower Floater with 10" Fawn. *Citron green, 14½" long, with sockets for three candles, late 1940's. Fawn has peg bottom with rubber washer for fit. $115.00– 145.00.*

Other colors: Crystal, twilight, copen blue.

Note: As of 1985, Summit Art Glass owns this mold. Referred to as "Chinese Modern Gazelle and Three-lite Flower Float."

Swan. *Light yellow/green, 6" long, blown hollow body with pulled neck, applied wings and tail. Rarity prohibits pricing.*

Other colors: Amethyst and cobalt.

Note: This swan has a closed back.

Tiffin Glassmasters, Book I, *permission given by Fred Bickenheuser.*

Shown here are a few of the Tiffin animals. The bulldog was made in black glass with satin finish, crystal with glass eyes. The second animal looks very much like a frog, but actually it is a cat candlestick. (Notice the paws. The tail comes down the long neck and shows on the back of the base of the candlestick.) Made in black with satin finish only, to our knowledge. The "Chessie" cat stands 11" high and was made in milk glass and black with satin finish. The smaller cat was made in the same colors as the large cat. Cat collectors have advised of finding other sizes of glass cats with this velvet satin finish, which was characteristic of Tiffin's production during this period of 1929–41.

Note: For small bulldog, see page 230.

Unidentified Owl. *Black satin, 7½" high.*
#9446 Small Cat. *Black satin (decorated), sometimes referred to as "Grotesque Cat," 1924. $85.00–125.00.*

186

#72 Frog Candlestick. *Black satin, 5½" high, 1924–34. Very rare. $65.00–85.00 each.*

Note: Also used as a child's napkin ring.

#9445 Cat. *Black satin, 6¼" high, raised bumps, 1924. Very rare. $95.00.*

187

The "Sassy Susie" cat was designed by master designer Reuben Haley and his son, Kenneth, in the 1900's. A search of the old mold inventories of the U.S. Glass Company indicates the mold was kept at Tiffin, and for a short period of time, at their Glassport, Pennsylvania plant, during the period when both factories were a part of the U.S. Glass Company. The cat was originally produced in white milk glass and black glass with a satin sheen finish. This particular satin finish is characteristic of Tiffin Glass only, and was used on many of their items during the Depression Era of 1929–1941.

When the Glassport factory was destroyed by fire in 1956, there were thousands of pieces of tooling that would have been buried forever, but Mr. Frank Fenton was a good friend of Mr. Carlson, Sr. (president of U.S. Glass Company) and he bought some of the tooling, the Sassy Susie cat being one. Also, Mr. Fenton stated that he would never make the cat in black satin or milk glass, being Tiffin's original colors.

This mold, now named "Alley Cat," was purchased by Fenton in 1960, appearing in regular production from 1970–73 in dark amethyst iridized glass. Production of the cat was once again planned for 1980 in Fenton's colonial blue with iridescent finish, for a private customer. See Fenton, page 63 for further colors. All production of Fenton's Alley Cat is so marked.

If you have a cat in either white milk glass, or black with a satin finish, you own a Tiffin glass animal!

"The weird feline holding down front cover position on the Outlook team this month has been christened 'Sassy Susie.'

Not because she makes audible remonstrance when left without food for days at a time, but because her expression has a meaning all its own. Makes a very efficient doorstop. Brightens dull corner. Sits pretty under a Christmas tree. Never fails to arouse comment when seen for the first time. Strong enough to be used as a means of defense, and if carried as a mascot on the briny deep, it could also be used to repel boarders.

All in all, 'Sassy Susie' has a real job in life cut out for her. Order by No. 9448."

(Reprinted through courtesy of Antique Publications, Marietta, Ohio.)

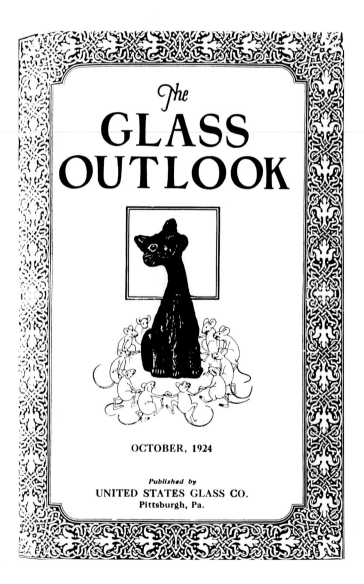

The
GLASS OUTLOOK

OCTOBER, 1924

Published by
UNITED STATES GLASS CO.
Pittsburgh, Pa.

Fish. Crystal, 8¾" high, 9" long, solid glass, 1935. $250.00–350.00.

#9448 Sassy Susie Cat. Black satin decorated, 11" high, circa 1900. $150.00–175.00.

Other colors: Milk glass.

Note: See page 63 for Fenton's Alley Cat.

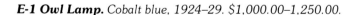

E-1 Owl Lamp. Cobalt blue, 1924–29. $1,000.00–1,250.00.

Note: Albino or milk glass (as shown in Bickenheuser's Tiffin Glassmasters, Book III, page 49), is the only one known. $1,000.00.

Viking Glass Company

Viking Glass Company logo showing original trademark.

Epic Line

While Viking's Epic Line extends beyond our Depression Era time frame, a book on glass animals would not be complete without the vibrantly colored animals of this line. The innovative design concept of the Epic Line is unlike any other!

From the late 1950's through the 1960's, Epic Line colors would include crystal, blunique (dark medium blue), persimmon, amberina, ebony, ruby, orchid, honey (amber), lime (vaseline), aqua blue, emerald, moss, and avocado green. The following pages are representative of the designs and colors of this line.

In 1988–91, Dalzell-Viking reissued some of the Epic animals in crystal, crystal frosted, and black. Signed "Dalzell," these animals are so noted in this chapter.

Items in this chapter preceded by double asterisk (**) are from a private collection and cannot be priced.

**Roses with Long Stems. Dark medium blue, ruby, moss green, and orange, solid glass, 4½" wide, 6" long.

Other colors: Crystal, amber, frosted amberina.

Note: Very scarce.

#1321 Epic Rooster. *9½"high, 1960's. Avocado, $35.00–55.00; ruby, $40.00–60.00; orange, $35.00–55.00.*

Other colors: Blunique (dark medium blue), $40.00–60.00; honey (amber), $35.00–55.00; persimmon (amberina), $40.00–60.00.

Reissues: Rooster made in limited production in 1978 in ruby and crystal.

#1311 Bird. *Orange, 9½" high, 1960's. $15.00–25.00.*
#1311 Bird. *Dark medium blue, 9½" high, 1960's. $15.00–25.00.*
#1310 Bird. *Ruby, 12" high, 1960's. $25.00–35.00.*
#1310 Bird. *Moss green, 12" high, 1960's. $15.00–25.00.*
#1311 Bird. *Orchid, 9½"high, 1960's. $20.00–30.00.*

Note: Also used as the finial on a two-piece candy box, #1311, 6" high. 1977–78 Viking catalog shows this bird in crystal and black. In 1991 this bird could be bought in black through the Viking outlet stores.

#1315 Egret. *Orange, dark medium blue, ruby, amber, ranging in height from 9½" to 12", depending on length of neck, 1960's. $35.00–45.00 each.*

Other colors: Made in Viking colors.

#1302 Horse. *Aqua blue, 11½" high, 1957. $75.00–95.00.*
#1302 Horse. *Amber, 11½" high, 1957. $75.00–95.00.*

Reissued: Reissued by Dalzell-Viking in crystal in 1989.

Note: See Paden City, page 169 for origin of this mold.

#6808 Rabbit. *Amber, 6½" high, 1960's. $25.00–35.00.*
#1301 Angelfish. *Amber, 6½" high, 1957. $55.00–75.00.*
#1301 Turtle. *Amber, 5½" long, 1957. $15.00–20.00.*

Other colors: Made in Viking colors. Angelfish made in milk glass, $55.00–75.00; ebony, $125.00–150.00; light blue, $100.00–125.00.

Reissues: Angelfish reissued by Dalzell-Viking in 1991 in crystal.

#1301 Angelfish. *Crystal, 6½" high, 1957. $55.00–75.00.*
#6808 Rabbit (a.k.a. Thumper). *Crystal, 6½" high, 1968. $25.00–35.00.*

Other colors: Made in Viking colors.

Reissues: Angelfish reissued by Dalzell-Viking in 1991 in crystal.

Note: See page 198 for special pour of rabbit.

193

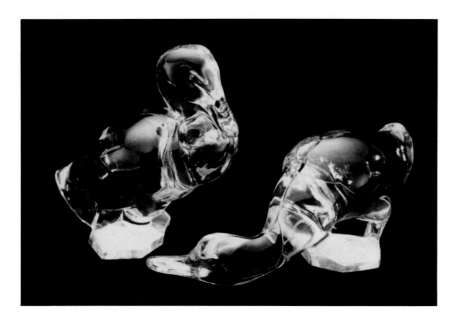

#6712 Fighting Ducks, Standing. *Crystal, 4½" high, 1967. $35.00–45.00.*
#6712 Fighting Ducks, Head Down. *Crystal, 2½" high, 1967. $35.00–45.00.*

Other colors: Made in Viking colors and tinted crystal.

Note: Made in ruby for only one year.

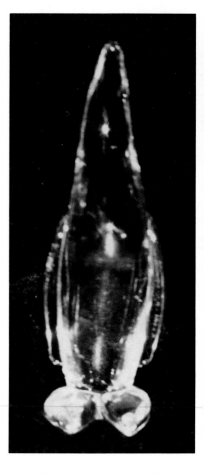

#1319 Penguin. *Crystal, 7" high, 1960's. $15.00–25.00.*

Other colors: Made in Viking colors.

Reissues: Dalzell-Viking in crystal, 1988.

#1320 Fish on Base. *Dark medium blue, 10" high, 1960's. $30.00–55.00.*

Other colors: Made in Viking colors.

#1317 Duck. *Ruby, 9" high, 1960's. $35.00–55.00.*
#1316 Duck. *Vaseline, 5" high, 1960's. $15.00–25.00.*

Other colors: Made in Viking colors.

Note: Small duck also used as finial in two-piece round candy box, #1313.

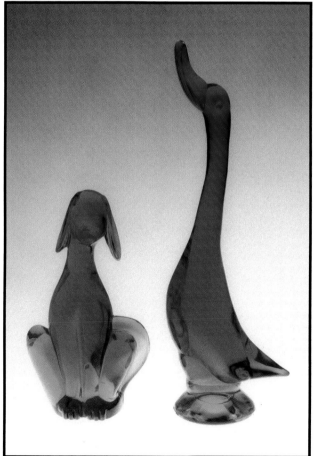

#1323 Dog. *Orange, 8" high, 1960's. $30.00–55.00.*
#1317 Duck, Head Up. *Orange, 13½" high, 1960's. $25.00–45.00.*

Other colors: Made in Viking colors.

Reissues: Dog reissued by Dalzell-Viking in crystal, 1990; in black, 1991.

#1322 Cat. *Green, 8" high, 1960's. $30.00–55.00.*
#6808 Rabbit. *Green, 6½" high, 1960's. $25.00–35.00.*

Other colors: Made in Viking colors.

Reissues: Cat reissued by Dalzell-Viking in crystal in 1990, in black in 1991.

**#6807 Bird. *Amber, 5" high, 1960's.*
** Rabbit on Scalloped Base. *Amber, 2½" high, 1960's.*

Other colors: Made in Viking colors.

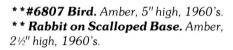

Seal. *Persimmon, 9¾" long. $10.00–15.00.*

Swan with Neck Pulled Up From Bowl. *Dark medium blue, 6½" long, scalloped bowl top. $20.00–30.00.*

"Wise Old Owl" on Log. *Amber, 5" high, flat-sided, weighs 5 lbs.! $15.00–20.00.*

**Bird. *Ruby, 4" high, 1960's.*
**Cat. *Ruby, 7" high, 1960's.*
**Whale. *Ruby, 5" long, 1960's.*

Other colors: Made in other Viking colors.

Viking Epic Line "Special Pour"

In 1978, the #6808 Rabbit was made for a private company in 500 each of the following colors: vaseline, blue milk glass, cobalt, custard, crystal, sapphire blue, green, pink, lime green slag, lemon custard slag, blue milk slag, and ruby.

The "Special Pour" bunnies are marked with a double "b" on the bottom as well as an incised rosette – distinguishing them from the Viking issue with a plain polished bottom.

Double "b" Bunnies. Custard, lemon custard slag, and sapphire blue, 6½" high, 1978. The original selling prices of these bunnies was $15.00 each.

Westmoreland Glass Company
Grapeville, Pennsylvania

#78 Bulldog Doorstop. *Golden sunset mist with green eyes, 8½" high, circa 1916. Weighs 5½ lbs. $350.00–450.00.*

Other colors: Black milk glass, white milk glass, black mist, brown mist, moss green, (jade reported in the 1930's). All of these colors are extremely rare and would fall into the $350.00– 450.00 price bracket.

Exceptionally rare is the circa 1925 bulldog with white head and black body. Beginning price for this fellow would be $1,000.00.

Made in black with gold collar in 1967. After 1984, made in cobalt and cobalt carnival by Summit Art Glass, with red collar and yellow rimmed eyes. See page 183.

Note: This bulldog mold was loaned by Westmoreland to Tiffin, and back to Westmoreland by the early 1940's. Collars on the Westmoreland dog were <u>brown leather</u>, originally, and in the 1920's, <u>brass spiked</u> collars were shown. In later years, a red leather collar was used.
    The bulldogs, being a large solid mass of glass, would tend to crack during the cooling process, leaving them in short supply.
    This mold now belongs to Summit Art Glass.

Originally this company was known as *Westmoreland Specialty Company*. Not only did this firm produce condiment jars, but condiments to fill them! Early on, glass items filled with candy were sold through the five-and-dime stores. Success in this endeavor led to other glassware lines, and in 1925, Westmoreland dropped the word "Specialty" and became known as the *Westmoreland Glass Company*. Early American patterns were reintroduced and their milk glass production was second to none. The covered animal dishes of Westmoreland, in all colors and slags, are eagerly sought after by today's collectors.
    In Westmoreland's early years, they produced a large selection of carnival glass (which was brought back in the 1970's in a variety of colors).
    Color arrived in the mid 1920's, including amber, green, blue, and roseline. Many items were made in crystal and hand-painted in color. Ebony, ruby, and marble glass were later colors. While Westmoreland colors were many beautiful shades, they remained famous for their milk glass production, considered the world's best. Westmoreland continued to make hand-made glassware of quality until its closing in 1984.
    Presently, much credit must be given to Phil, Helen, and P.J. Rosso, Jr., operating under the name of *Wholesale Glass Dealers* in Port Vue, Pennsylvania, for making "Westmoreland" happen again. The Rossos, in addition to reactivating a number of old Westmoreland molds, have been instrumental in forming the National Westmoreland Glass Collectors Club, a separate entity, which puts out the Towne Crier newsletter and holds a yearly convention. In addition, the Rossos have established a Westmoreland Glass Museum in their area. The Rosso's trademark is an "R" within the keystone shape.
    Westmoreland molds are now owned by several different companies such as:

Dalzell-Viking — no marks, paper labels only
Fenton Art Glass Company — always marked with Fenton logo
Plum Glass — "PG" within the keystone symbol
Rosso Wholesale Glass Dealers — "R" within the keystone symbol
Treasured Editions, Ltd. — Hand-painted pieces are dated after Westmorelands closing

Summit Art Glass — "V" in a circle, is listed as having the following animal molds:
2½" Wren
2" Chickadee
1½" Butterfly
2½" Butterfly
4" Butterfly
3½" Turtle Flower Frog
8½" Bulldog Doorstop
5" Starfish Candleholder
1000 Eye Turtle & Ashtray

Any, or all of these companies (except Fenton) may leave the "W" over "G" mark on these pieces. Also utilized is the Westmoreland mark in a circular fashion.

A very special thanks to Lorraine Kovar and P.J. Rosso, Jr. for all their help!

Westmoreland Glass Company Color Chart

Westmoreland's color production was vast and varied – as were their hand-decorated items. The following chart is representative of this company's colors:

Almond, clear or mist
Amber, clear or mist
Amethyst
Black Milk Glass
Black Mist
Blue, Antique, clear or mist
Blue, Bermuda
Blue, Brandywine
Blue, Cobalt, carnival
Blue, dark mist
Blue, Electric, carnival
Blue, Ice, clear or carnival
Coral, mist
Coraline, soft mist
Crystal, clear/mist/flashed color
Flame, clear or mist
Golden Sunset, clear or mist

Green, emerald, carnival
Green Marble
Green, Mint, opaque
Green, Laurel
Honey carnival
Lilac, mist/opalescent/pastel
Pink, clear/mist/pastel
Pink carnival
Purple carnival
Purple marble
Ruby, clear/stained/carnival
Vaseline, clear or mist
White Milk Glass
White Milk, mother-of-pearl
Yellow, clear or mist

Note: The smaller animals shown on pages 201–202 were made in most of Westmoreland's clear and/or mist colors, as well as a few carnival colors.
Westmoreland refers to their frosted issue as "mist," and their slag issue as "marble."

"Our glass menagerie has a charming history, as many of our current animals date back to the 18th century when we first began making glass. Back then, these covered animal dishes were packed full of mustard or jelly, and then sealed with parafin. Our Animal Kingdom no longer comes with condiments, but still is as popular as ever . . ."

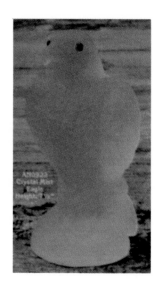

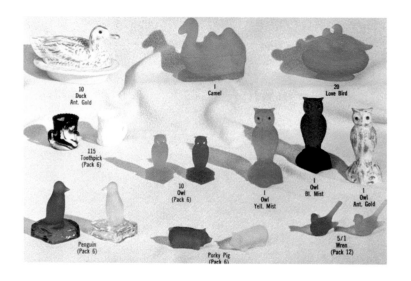

#75 *Small Bulldog.* *Black mist, gold painted collar and rhinestone eyes, 2½" high, circa 1910. $25.00–35.00.*
#75 *Small Bulldog.* *Crystal mist, gold painted collar and rhinestone eyes, 2½" high, circa 1910. $25.00–35.00.*

Other colors: Early colors: Crystal mist, crystal, black mist, black. Later colors: Milk glass, black milk glass, black frosted milk glass, golden sunset, moss green, ruby, carnival, electric blue carnival. Possible to find in any Westmoreland color. All colors $25.00–35.00, ruby carnival higher.

Reissues: Reissued by Rosso Wholesale Glass Dealers after Westmoreland closed in 1984. Colors would include vaseline, cobalt, ruby, black amethyst, milk glass, black with red accents, white with red accents, cobalt with white collar, blue ice, blue ice carnival, blue slag, pink, custard, cranberry, and cranberry ice carnival. Reissued in 1992 in green opalescent and green opalescent iridized. Recently reissued by Plum Glass Company in black satin and milk glass.

Note: *This small bulldog is also shown in* Tiffin Glass I, *page 57 and also in* Fenton Glass First 25 Years, *page 113, item #307. See Comparison Sheet, page 230.*

#9 *Pouter Pigeon.* *2½" high, 1" ground bottom, 1970's. Crystal, $17.00–22.00; pink mist, blue mist, apricot mist, $25.00–30.00 each.*

Other colors: 1971 – amber, blue, green mist, lilac, lilac mist, dark blue mist, pink mist. 1984 – black (experimental).

#2 Small Butterfly. *Green mist, 2½" wide. $18.00–22.00.*
#2 Small Butterfly. *Blue mist, 2½" wide. $18.00–22.00.*
#3 Large Butterfly. *Crystal, 4½" wide. $22.00–27.00.*

Other colors: #2 Butterfly: Crystal, mint green, green, light and dark blue, pink, apricot and yellow mists, mint green, pink opaque carnival, yellow opaque, purple carnival, pink, almond, cobalt carnival. Smoke grey and pink mist (possibly others) reissued. #3 Butterfly: Pink, yellow, antique blue and brown mists, purple marble, brown marble, antique blue, almond, mint green, and vaseline. Carnival and marble colors, $25.00–35.00.

Reissues: 1977 limited edition in purple carnival for The Historical Glass Museum Foundation.

Note: Large Butterfly #3 also came with peg to fit into tree stump base.

#7/1 Robin. *Crystal, 3¼" long, no base, 1" ground bottom. $15.00–20.00.*
#11 Cardinal. *Green mist. $15.00–20.00.*

Other colors: Robin: Crystal, antique blue, milk glass, almond, pink mist, antique blue milk glass mist, reissued in cobalt. Cardinal: Crystal, ruby, purple marble, dark blue mist, light blue mist, apricot mist, and ruby carnival, reissued in ruby, purple carnival, orange slag, and cobalt. Carnival and marble colors, $22.50.

Note: Robin also made in larger size, 5⅛" long.

204

#1063 Starfish Candleholder. *Almond, 5" wide. Pair, $25.00–30.00.*

Other colors: Crystal mist, milk glass, antique blue mist, almond, antique blue clear, milk glass mother-of-pearl. Colored opaques or milk glass priced higher.

Note: All colors scarce. Manufactured with dolphin line.

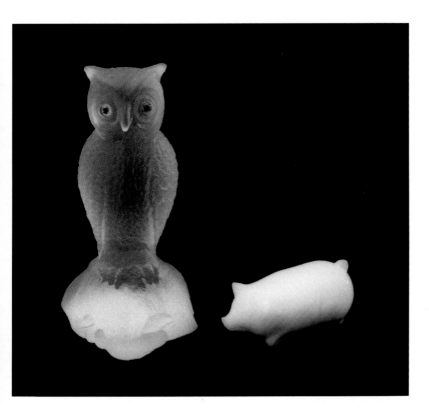

#1 Owl with Glass Eyes. *Crystal mist, 5½" high, grassy base with mushrooms. $25.00–30.00.*
Porky Pig. *Milk glass, 3" long, 1½" wide, no base and hollow, late 1970's – early 1980's. $10.00–15.00.*

Other colors: Owl: mid 1970's, early 1980's, amber mist, dark blue, antique gold, topaz, purple marble, caramel mother-of-pearl, antique blue mist, yellow mist, and almond mist. 1980's, Crystal mother-of-pearl, almond mother-of-pearl, milk glass with 22kt. gold feathers, milk glass, ruby, ruby carnival. Carnival and marble colors priced higher. Reissued in cobalt and rubina. Porky Pig: Crystal mist, dark blue mist, mint green, milk glass, yellow opaque, cobalt carnvial, blue opaque, and ruby. Reissued in cobalt, milk glass, milk glass with mother-of-pearl, some pieces hand-painted.

Note: It is possible to find the owl in several colors not found in books, as it was heavily produced for gift shops.

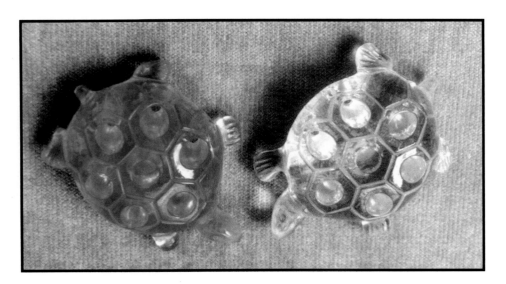

#1860 Turtle Flower Block. *4" long, <u>7 holes</u>, 1924. Crystal and green, $45.00–55.00 each.*

Reissues: Reissued from Westmoreland mold, since its 1984 closing, in cobalt, mother-of-pearl, amethyst, and milk glass. In 1970, was reissued as #10 paperweight (no holes) in green, lilac, and dark blue mists. See below.

#10 Paperweight. *Green mist, 4" long, <u>no holes</u>, 1970. $20.00–25.00.*

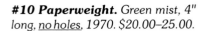

1,000 Eye Turtle, Two-Piece Cigarette Box. *Crystal with flashed dots of ruby, lavender, and pale yellow, 7¾" long. $45.00–55.00.*

Other colors: Crystal, white milk glass, black milk glass, golden sunset, moss green, and olive green.

Reissues: Reissued after Westmoreland closed in: amberina, cobalt blue, mother-of-pearl, amethyst, light blue, white milk glass, blue milk glass, orange, and some with hand-painted decorations.

Note: Set also included two small ashtrays, 4¼" long. $10.00–15.00 each.

1,000 Eye Turtle, Two-Piece Cigarette Box. *Black, 7¾" long. $40.00–45.00. Accompanying ashtrays, black, 4¼" long. $10.00–15.00 each.*

Bird In Flight. *Amber marigold, wing out-stretched 4¼" long, 5" wing spread, before 1960's label. $20.00–30.00.*

#5 Two-Piece Wren on Perch. *Light blue mist wren on milk glass base. Wren has peg bottom which fits into branch. $25.00–35.00.*

Other colors: Wren: Pink mist, green mist, dark blue mist, apricot mist, almond, black milk glass. Base: black milk glass, brown "wood-like" treatment.

Penguin on Ice Floe. *Brandywine blue mist. $30.00–35.00.*

Other colors: Crystal mist with a plain crystal ice floe.

Note: Rumor has it this fellow was made for a Kool cigarette advertisement.

Owl Bookend. *On curved-front base with three books on end behind owl, circa 1926. Crystal, $65.00–75.00 each; colors, $75.00–100.00 each.*

Lorraine Kovar tells us: "I believe this is the only catalog to ever show this owl bookend . . . I have never seen one, otherwise I would own it! From the 1926 era, it is likely that it might be found in Roseline (pink), amber, and perhaps many other colors. I don't imagine many of these survived because glass is slippery, and, if the books fell over – CRASH!"

Note: Our research has failed to turn up any additional information on this design. The ad mentioned appeared in Hazel Marie Weatherman's Book II.

No. 10 Owl on Two Books. *With rhinestone eyes, 3½" high, circa 1926. Usually contains the "WG" mark. $25.00–30.00. Carnival colors, $30.00–35.00.*

Other colors: 1960's and 1970's: Green mist, dark blue mist, light blue mist, yellow mist, apricot mist, almond, antique blue, mint green, yellow opaque, pink opaque, blue opaque, cobalt carnival, electric blue carnival, ruby carnival, purple marble, ruby, brandywine blue, black milk glass, white milk glass, possible to find in any of this company's colors as well as slags. Later issues of this owl after Westmoreland's closing in 1984 would include black milk glass, cobalt, cobalt carnival, vaseline, vaseline carnival, ruby, ruby carnival, pink milk glass, pink frosted, blue ice, blue ice carnival, milk glass mother-of-pearl, caprice blue, lime green, blue frost, blue, amber, milk glass, pink.

Note: Degenhart made almost an identical owl in many colors. It is usually marked with a "D" in a heart.

Who Done It?

Piranha Fish. *Bubbly texture, 4½" high, solid glass with good detail.*
Owl Flower Frog. *Amber with rhinestone eyes, 4½" high, circa 1928. Also seen in rose and green.*
Hen. *Yellow, 3" high, solid with polished bottom.*

Continued research has failed to turn up the parentage of the animals shown in this chapter. We would appreciate reader input on *Who Done It?* Price-wise, the market would call for whatever the buyer is willing to pay!

Dog on Triangular Penholder Base. *Pink frosted, 4½" high.*
Duck. *Pink, 2½" high, open back.*

Dog. *Small doxy, amber, 2" high.*
Muddlers. *Amber, with eagle heads, stirrer, 4¾" long; spoon, 5¼" long.*

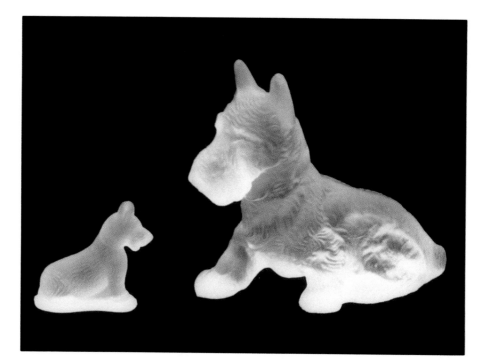

Miniature Scottie. *Frosted crystal, 2"*
high. (L.E. Smith).
Large Scottie. *Frosted crystal, 4½"*
high. Not L.E. Smith.

Note: *L. E. Smith large scottie has*
tail out straight.

Rabbit. *Crystal, 5" high, solid glass.*

Note: *Found in Mosser 1984*
catalog.

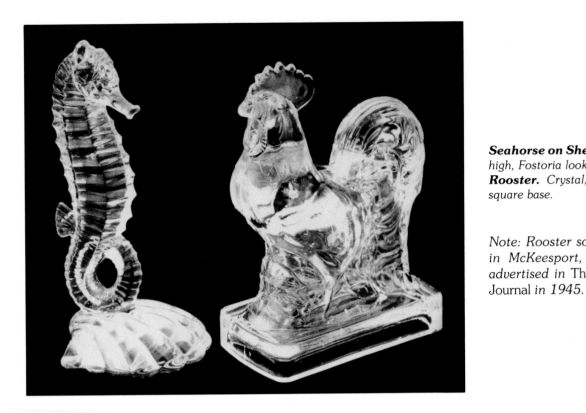

Seahorse on Shell Base. *Crystal, 8¼"
high, Fostoria look-alike.*
Rooster. *Crystal, 8" high, hollow on
square base.*

Note: Rooster sold through Sabin's
in McKeesport, Pennsylvania and
advertised in The Crockery & Glass
Journal in 1945.

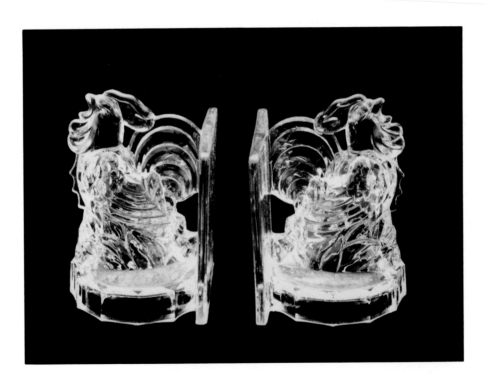

Rooster Bookends. *Crystal, 5¾" high, hollow, rounded base with 10 indents.*

Rearing Horse Bookends. *Crystal, hollow, rounded base with 10 indents.*

Note: Also made with anchors and leaping gazelles on the same style base.

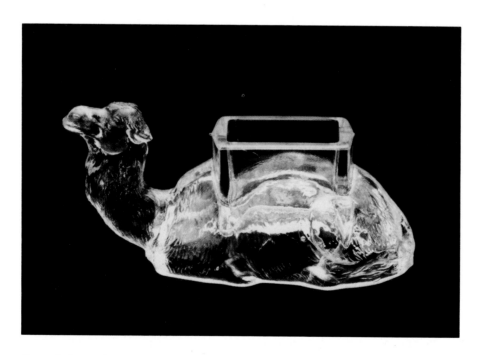

Camel, Lying Down. *Crystal, 7½" long, circa 1928. Hollow place on back will hold pack of cigarettes.*

213

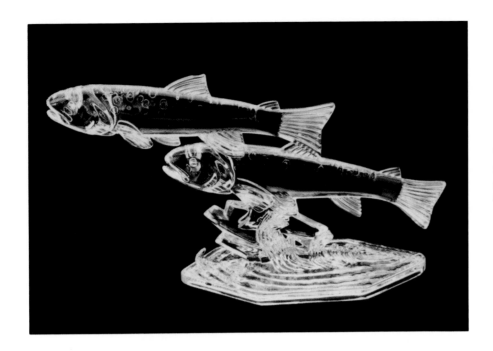

Trout or Walleye. *Crystal, each fish measures 8", the elongated diamond base is 7" long. Fish have raised spots and are swimming through seaweed.*

Fish. *Crystal, 5¾" high, 8" long, on hollow base of waves, has been drilled for a lamp base.*

Pheasant. *Crystal, 13" long, 9" high, open back, great feather detail, diamond-shaped base.*

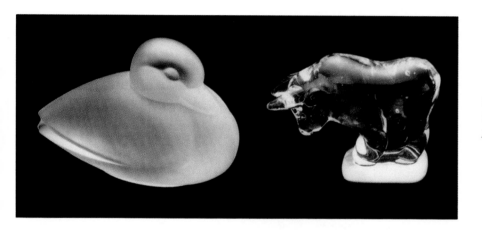

Duck. *Frosted crystal, 3" high, solid.*
Bull. *Crystal, 2½" high, 3½" long, solid, polished bottom.*

Donkey. *Crystal, 3¾" high, 5¼" long, solid, flat-sided.*
Goldfish. *Crystal, 2½" high, solid.*

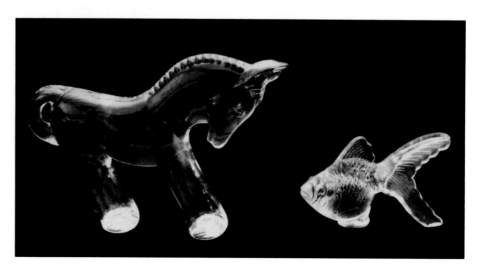

215

Rooster. *Crystal, 9½" high, 10½" wide, solid, excellent detail.*

Rooster Candleholder. *Crystal with frosted comb and wattle, 6" high.*

Grouse. *Crystal, 5½" high, 5" wide, solid.*

Fish. *Crystal, 8" high, solid glass, circa 1935.*

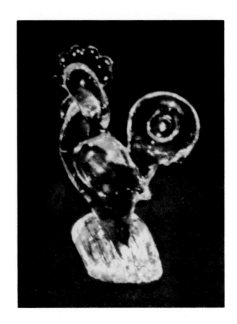

Rooster with Curled Tail. *Crystal, 6¾" high.*

Rooster. *Frosted with clear crystal comb and base sides, 7½" high.*

Swan with Three Tier Lattice on Back. *Crystal, 10½" high.*

Note: Originally thought to be Duncan-Miller private mold work, but has not been documented as such. Also made with two tier lattice, 7" high.

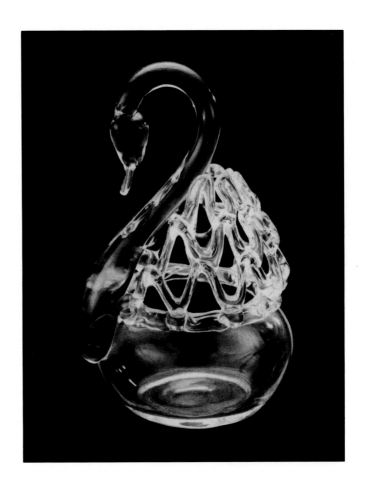

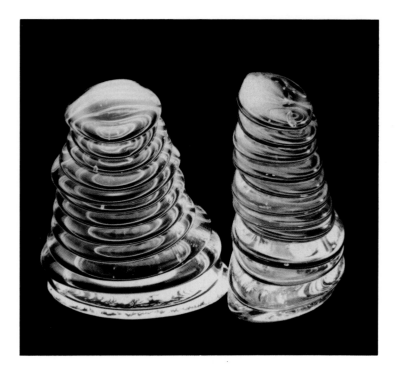

Spiral Bookends. *Crystal, 6½" high, solid.*

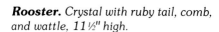

Rooster. *Crystal with ruby tail, comb, and wattle, 11½" high.*

Other colors: All crystal.

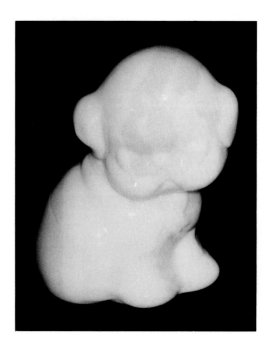

Sitting Pug Dog. *Milk glass, 5¼" high, solid.*

Other colors: Honey, onyx, dark green, dark ruby, and milk glass. Some of the pugs were hand-decorated and had ribbons around their neck.

Note: Also seen in decorated milk glass as electric night light, on round black base, 6½" with base.
William Heacock says in The Glass Collector, *Issue #4, Fall 1982:*
"This adorable decorated milk glass puppy dog electric night lamp is a real mystery. It is not U.S. Glass, as the base is different from those shown in BTG2, p. 72. The electric fixtures date it from about 1920. I suspect it was made by Consolidated Lamp & Glass, as the decoration reminds me of the Santa Claus night lamp . . ."

Dirigible Fish Aquarium. *Crystal, 18"
long.*

Note: William Heacock said in the Glass
Review, *March 1981:*
*"Fortunately one factory saw fit to
create a tribute to the dirigible, in the
form of a fish bowl – (seen at a show in
Livonia, Michigan). On the left are the
tail and rudder, at the base is the
observation deck . . ."*

Elephant. *Black milk
glass, 3¼" high, solid.*

Goldfish Candleholders. *Frosted pink, 4½" high.*

Turtle. *Pink, 4" long, great detail, solid with
slight hollow underneath.*

Miscellaneous

Note: Items in this chapter preceded by double asterisk (**) are from a private collection and cannot be priced. We could not pass up the opportunity to share these animals with you!

L.G. Wright Glass Company
New Martinsville, West Virginia

#70-12 Large Two-Piece Turtle. *Amber, 10" long. $65.00–85.00.*

Other colors: Crystal, dark emerald green, chocolate.

Note: This turtle is referred to as the "Belfast" turtle in HMW-2, of unknown parentage. We are happy to find his home at last. L.G. Wright has definitely confirmed this turtle to be theirs!
Wright Glass catalogs show a wide variety of colored glass, lamps, Victorian glass, moon & stars, and early American patterns.
Wright informs us that their two-piece turtle dish is presently being made in crystal only.

Summit Art Glass Company
Rootstown, Ohio

Polar Bear. *Blue frosted, 4½" high. Market price.*

Note: Summit Art Glass, founded by Russell Vogelsong and wife Joann, produce lovely novelty ware, and some new glass from old molds, purchased from defunct glass companies of the past.
This polar bear is like Fostoria's bear, but with round base instead of square. See page 76.

Gillinder & Sons
Philadelphia, Pennsylvania

**Large Buddha. *Flame, 6½" high.*
** Small Buddha. *Vaseline, 4½" high.*

Note: Gillinder & Sons founded in 1867, and became part of the U.S. Glass merger in 1891.
The major differences between Gillinder and small Cambridge Buddhas would be:
1. Cambridge Buddha has beaded hat, with topknot and large hanging earrings, Gillinder has neither.
2. Cambridge has front scalloped base with round pedestal underneath, while Gillinder has flat base.
See Cambridge, page 40.

Federal Glass Company
Columbus, Ohio

#2563 Horse Head. *Crystal, 5½" high, hollow, sometimes filled with candy, having a cardboard bottom.* $10.00–15.00.
#2565 "Mopey" Dog. *Crystal, 3½" high.* $5.00–10.00.

Note: Beginning in 1900 as a hand-operated glass house, changing to automation by the 1920's. Federal became a major supplier of restaurants, motels, etc., and pioneered the decorated tumbler. The company became a division of Federal Paper Board Company in 1958.

Owens-Illinois Glass Company
Toledo, Ohio

**Gazelle Bookend. *Frosted crystal.*

Note: Owens Bottle Machine Company founded in 1903, merged with Illinois Glass Company in 1929, and became Owens-Illinois. Under ownership of Libbey Glass Company since 1936.

Rodifer Glass Company
Bellaire, Ohio

**Bear On Cake of Ice. *Crystal, 9½" high. (Made for Imperial Glass Festival in Bellaire, Ohio.) Very rare.*

Note: Rodifer Glass Company was mostly noted for its commercial opalware gearshift knobs for automobiles, silicon shields for gas wells, and opalware blanks for Wavecrest.

Silverbrook Art Glass
New York

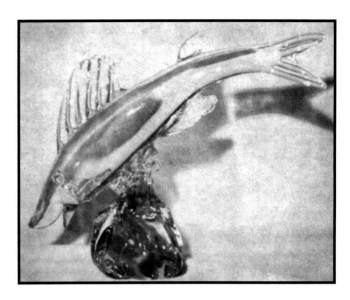

**Fish, Head Up. *Crystal, 8½" high.*
**Fish, Head Down. *Crystal, 8" high, 11" long.*

Blenko Glass Company
Milton, West Virginia

Ram's Head Solid Glass Paperweight. *Cobalt blue, 6" high. Market price.*

Note: Beginning in 1922, this company is enjoying success on today's market with a wide line of stylized glassware.

Pilgrim Glass Corporation
Ceredo, West Virginia

The following three glass animals are the creation of Alessandro and Robert Moretti, designers and glass blowers for Pilgrim Glass Corporation. Founded in 1950, and currently in business, their specialty is quality hand-blown glassware.

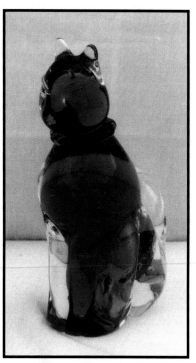

Above left: ****Angelfish.** *Emerald green with orange mouth, 9" high.*

Above right: ****Cat.** *Crystal and cobalt combination, with ruby collar and nose, 7" high.*

Right: ****Standing Grouse.** *Crystal and emerald green combination, 11" high.*

Aladdin Lamps

G335C Hoppy Horse Head. Alacite, 1951. $400.00 (with original shade).

Note: The Mantle Lamp Company of America began operations in 1908 with kerosene burning lamps being their main production until the 1940's (even with electric lamps in the picture). Aladdin Lamps became their tradename, and the collectible lamps of today were made in Alexandria, Indiana. In 1949, they moved operations to Nashville, Tennessee. "Alacite" was introduced in 1939.

G-234 Golden Pheasant. Alacite glass, 1941. $175.00.

Rooster Lamp. *Crystal, 1936. $1,000.00.*

G-16 Figurine. *Alacite, 5-ring base, 1940. $650.00.*

Note: Also made in "Opalique," which is a bright clear glass, almost luminescent, finished with a smooth satin etch – quite different from Aladdin's crystal with a satin finish, which appears almost "opaque."

Steuben Glassworks
Corning, New York

**#7231 Elephant. *8" high.*
**#6495 Kneeling Lady. *7½" high.*
**#7133 Alabaster Lady. *9" high*
**#7064 Double Fish. *7½" high.*
**#7039 Lady in Circle. *9½" high.*

Note: The above flower frogs are in a satin finish, (with the exception of the alabaster lady). All figurines have peg bottoms which fit into their hand-blown crystal bases. Steuben Glassworks was founded by a group of men which included Frederick Carder and T. Hawkes, in 1903. Steuben, presently in operation, is well-known for their magnificent art glass creations!

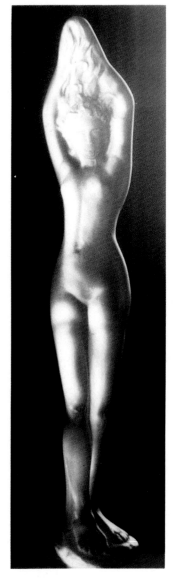

**#6483 Diving Lady. *Satin finish, 13½" high.*

Note: Figurine is on peg which fits into her hand-blown crystal base.

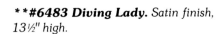

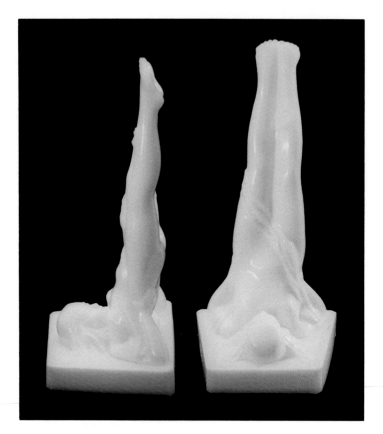

Mosser Glass Company

Ladyleg Bookend. *Custard, late 1970's. Original selling price, $150.00–175.00 pair.*

Note: Produced in the original Cambridge mold. They were also made in green iridized and sold for $30.00 per pair. Mosser Glass Company also produced the Ladyleg Bookend Commemorative item in medium blue during 1977 for the National Cambridge Collectors, Inc.

Siamese Swans

The Siamese Twin Swans is purported to be some of Duncan & Miller Glass Company's private mold work. It was made for a company in New York and was never sold as a line product. Rarity prohibits pricing.

Hocking/Anchor Hocking

Hocking Glass Company began in Lancaster, Ohio in 1905, making small wares mostly by hand. Hocking acquired subsidiaries in the 1920's, and claims the first glass baby food jar. Numerous glass houses were assumed by Hocking in the early years, and in 1969, the name was changed to Anchor Hocking Corporation.

Pachyderm. *Green, 4⅜" high, 6" long, two-piece, circa mid 1920's. From a private collection.*

Pachyderm. *Rose, 4⅜" high, 6" long, two-piece, circa 1926. From a private collection.*

Other colors: Vitrock and crystal.

Verlys

Duck on Shallow Dish. *Resembles a pond with waves, crystal with satin finish, 4½" high, 5" long.*

Note: This mold was purchased by Fenton in 1968, and subsequently reissued bearing the Fenton oval logo.

Verlys . . . an art glass of crystal with acid-finished relief work, originally produced by Verlys of France. In 1935, Holophane Company of Newark, Ohio (primarily a glass lamp fixture company) produced Verlys as an American branch of the French company. In 1957, Holophane gave the A.H. Heisey Company permission to produce some items for them. Heisey produced 19 items, none of which were signed, and only those items made in the limelight color can be verified as Heisey. Verlys is sometimes marked by "script scratched" signature, or impressed in the mold.

229

Small Bulldog Comparison . . . The Mystery Deepens!

P.J. Rosso, of Wholesale Glass Dealers, tells us that when going to the old Westmoreland plant to purchase the small bulldog mold, he noticed _two_ small bulldog molds. As one was incomplete, he didn't examine it, and couldn't say which side the collar buckled on. He purchased, and has since reissued, the small bulldog mold as we know it today.

Another source indicates there were also _two_ molds for Tiffin's small bulldog.

It is the author's opinion, based on extensive research, that definite differences are apparent between the Tiffin and Westmoreland small bulldogs, indicating there would have been two or more molds, as opposed to Tiffin having borrowed Westmoreland's mold (as was the case with the large bulldog).

1. The collar of the Westmoreland pup is wider and always buckles on the left side, while Tiffin's buckles on the right and has a narrower collar.
2. From the back, the Westmoreland dog appears to be slouched more to the side than Tiffin's dog.
3. The chin line is slightly longer on the Westmoreland dog.

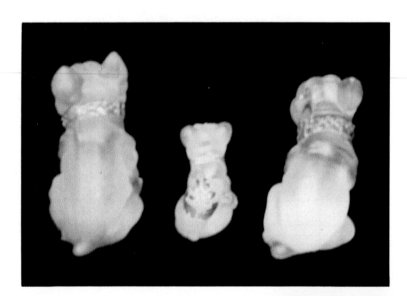

Tip: A check of original colors, as well as reissue colors, listed in both chapters, will help the collector to identify their dog!

Tiffin's Small Bulldog.
Import Pup, souvenir of Canada.
Westmoreland's Small Bulldog.

Westmoreland's Small Bulldog.
Right front paw missing.
Tiffin's Small Bulldog.

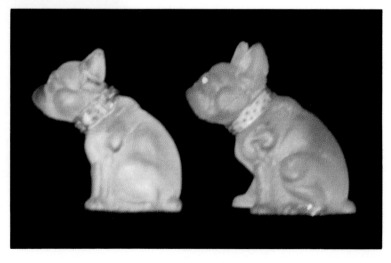

Comparison For Rearing Horse Bookends

There were four companies that made Rearing Horse Bookends, and they are easily confused. First, let's dispense with the one made by Heisey. It is much different than the other three. The easiest way to tell is by the flowing mane and the nose and head high in the air. For photo and complete details on the Heisey horse, see page 96.

Left to right: L.E. Smith, Fostoria, and New Martinsville.

Bottom view.

The horse made by L.E. Smith is 8" tall, 5¾" long. It is easy to tell from the remaining three by simply looking at the mane. It is the only one of the four that is beaded. $20.00–30.00.

The horse made by Fostoria is 7¾" tall with a 5½" long base. It has a close-cropped mane and like the other three, has the front legs folded under. Unique to the Fostoria horse is the rectangular opening on the bottom of the base. It measures 4½" long, 2¼" wide, ⅛" deep. This creates a ledge before the start of the hollow in the animal. A small but notable feature is that the right ear is smaller than the left. $35.00–45.00.

The New Martinsville horse is 7½" tall and the base is 5½" long. It has a close-cropped mane and a flowing tail like the other three. The clarity of glass in the New Martinsville horse is better than that of Fostoria. The bottom of the base is ground smooth <u>to the hollow</u> which goes up into the animal. $65.00–75.00.

Sources

A Guide for Study of Fostoria	*Milbra Long*
Aladdin Electric Lamps	*J.W. Courter*
American Glass Animals A to Z	*Evelyn Zemel*
Animal Kingdom in Treasured Glass	*Mary Van Pelt and Wanda Huffman*
Colors in Cambridge Glass	*Cambridge Collectors of America*
Daze Past	*Betty Bell*
Depression Era Glass II	*Hazel Marie Weatherman*
Depression Glass III	*Sandra Stout*
Encyclopedia of Duncan Glass	*Gail Krause*
Handmade Duncan Catalog #89	*Gail Krause*
Heisey Glass, Vol. 1–4	*Clarence W. Vogel*
Fantastic Figurines	*Mary Van Pelt*
Fenton, First 25 Years	*William Heacock*
Figurines in Crystal	*Mary Van Pelt*
Glass Collector's Almanac	*Betty Newbound*
Glass Collector, Issue #4, 1982	*William Heacock*
Glass Review *and/or* Rainbow Review	*Gwen Shumpert*
Glass Review, Rainbow Review, Glass Review Volumes I, II, & III	*Barbara Shaeffer, Publisher and Editor*
Heisey By Imperial	*Heisey Collectors of America*
New Martinsville, Volumes I & II	*Addie & Everett Miller*
Phoenix & Consolidated Art Glass, 1928–1980	*Jack D. Wilson*
Tiffin Glassmasters, Books I, II, & III	*Fred Bickenheuser*
Westmoreland Glass	*Lorraine Kovar*

Periodicals

The Towne Crier	*Westmoreland Glass Collectors Club*
Crystal Ball	*Cambridge Collectors, Inc.*
Tiffin Glassmasters	*Tiffin Glass Collectors Club*
Heisey News	*Heisey Collectors of America*
Facets of Fostoria	*Fostoria Glass Society*
Duncan Glass Journal	*National Duncan Glass Society*
The Daze	*Teri Steel, Publisher and Editor*
The Collector	*Lois Bowman, Publisher and Editor*
Glass Collector's Digest	*Antique Publications*

National Glass Organization Directory

Reprinted through courtesy of Antique Publications, Marietta, Ohio.

Fenton Art Glass Collectors
P.O. Box 384
Williamstown, WV 26187

Glass Knife Collectors Club
P.O. Box 342
Los Alamitos, CA 90720

The Fostoria Glass Society
P.O. Box 826
Moundsville, WV 26041

Glass Museum Foundation
1157 N. Orange Box 921
Redlands, CA 92373

Int. Carnival Glass Association
Lee Markley, Secretary
R.R. #1 Box 14
Mentone, IN 46539

Cambridge Collectors Inc.
P.O. Box 416
Cambridge, OH 43725

Candlewick Club
c/o Virginia R. Scott
275 Milledge Terrace
Athens, GA 30606

National Greentown Glass
Jerry D. Garrett, Planner
1807 West Madison Street
Kokomo, IN 46901

Milk Glass Collectors
c/o Arlene Johnson
1113 Birchwood Drive
Garland, TX 75043

Glass Collectors Club of Toledo
c/o 2727 Middlesex Drive
Toledo, OH 43606

American Carnival Glass Assoc.
Dennis Runk
P.O. Box 235
Littlestown, PA 17340

Marble Collector's Society
P.O. Box 222
Trumbull, CT 06611

H.C. Fry Glass Society
P.O. Box 41
Beaver, PA 15009

Collectible Carnival Glass Assoc.
Wilma Thurston
2360 N. Old S.R. 9
Columbus, IN 47203

New England Carnival Glass Club
Eva Backer, Membership
12 Sherwood Road
West Hartford, CT 06117

**National Depression Glass
Association**
P.O. Box 69843
Odessa, TX 79769

**Old Morgantown Glass Collector's
Guild**
P.O. Box 894
Morgantown, WV 26507

**National Imperial Glass Collectors
Society**
P.O. Box 534
Bellaire, OH 43906

National Duncan Glass Society
P.O. Box 965
Washington, PA 15301

Tiffin Glass Collectors Club
P.O. Box 554
Tiffin, OH 44883

Aladdin Knights
c/o J.W. Courter
Route 1
Simpson, IL 62985

**Heart of America Carnival Glass
Association**
C. Lucile Britt
3048 Tamarak Drive
Manhattan, KS 66502

Paperweight Collectors
P.O. Box 468
Garden City Park, NY 11010

Toothpick Holder Collectors
Joyce Ender, Membership
Red Arrow Hwy., P.O. Box 246
Sawyer, MI 49125

Glass Research Society of New Jersey
Wheaton Village
Millville, NJ 08332

National Early American Glass Club
Attn: Membership Chairman
P.O. Box 8489
Silver Spring, MD 20907

Stretch Glass Society
Joanne Rodgers
P.O. Box 770643
Lakewood, OH 44107

American Cut Glass Association
1603 SE 19th, Suite 112
Edmond, OK 73013

Pairpoint Cup Plate Collectors
Box 52D
East Weymouth, MA 02189

**Antique and Art Glass Salt Shaker
Collectors Society**
2832 Rapidan Trail
Maitland, FL 32751

The Corning Museum of Glass
Director of Public Programs
One Museum Way
Corning, NY 14830–2253

Perfume and Scent Bottle Collectors
Jeanne Parris
2022 E. Charleston Blvd.
Las Vegas, NV 89104

Heisey Collectors of America, Inc.
Box 4367
Newark, OH 43055

**National Westmoreland Glass
Collectors Club**
P.O. Box 372
Export, PA 15632

National Bottle Museum
20 Church Avenue
Ballston Spa, NY 12020

National Fenton Glass Society
P.O. Box 4008
Marietta, OH 45750

Collectors of Findlay Glass
P.O. Box 256
Findlay, OH 45839–0256

Update . . . "Heisey Gold"

In March of 1992, the Heisey Collectors of America announced their plans to issue the "Gold Animal Collector's Series." This Series will be made by Fenton Art Glass Company in their roseline color.

The set consists of the following twelve animals:

1.	Head Forward Filly	7.	Airedale
2.	Standing Duckling	8.	Standing Colt
3.	Fish Bookend	9.	Giraffe
4.	Rabbit Paperweight	10.	Tiger Paperweight
5.	Gazelle	11.	Hen
6.	Cygnet	12.	Sow

This "Gold Series" will be limited to 450 sets and each set will be numbered. Issue price is $600.00 per set.

Photo Index

Books on Antiques and Collectibles

Most of the following books are available from your local book seller or antique dealer, or on loan from your public library. If you are unable to locate certain titles in your area you may order by mail from COLLECTOR BOOKS, P.O. Box 3009, Paducah, KY 42002-3009. This is only a partial listing of the books on antiques that are available from Collector Books. All books are well illustrated and contain current values. Add $2.00 for postage for the first book ordered and $.30 for each additional book. Include item number, title and price when ordering. Allow 14 to 21 days for delivery

BOOKS ON GLASS AND POTTERY

1810 American Art Glass, Shuman $29.95
2016 Bedroom & Bathroom Glassware of the Depression Years . $19.95
1312 Blue & White Stoneware, McNerney $9.95
1959 Blue Willow, 2nd Ed., Gaston $14.95
2270 Collectible Glassware from the 40's, 50's, & 60's, Florence . $19.95
3311 Collecting Yellow Ware - Id. & Value Gd., McAllister .$16.95
2352 Collector's Ency. of Akro Agate Glassware, Florence .$14.95
1373 Collector's Ency. of American Dinnerware, Cunningham .$24.95
2272 Collector's Ency. of California Pottery, Chipman $24.95
3312 Collector's Ency. of Children's Dishes, Whitmyer $19.95
2133 Collector's Ency. of Cookie Jars, Roerig $24.95
2273 Collector's Ency. of Depression Glass, 10th Ed., Florence ..$19.95
2209 Collector's Ency. of Fiesta, 7th Ed., Huxford $19.95
1439 Collector's Ency. of Flow Blue China, Gaston $19.95
1915 Collector's Ency. of Hall China, 2nd Ed., Whitmyer ..$19.95
2334 Collector's Ency. of Majolica Pottery, Katz-Marks $19.95
1358 Collector's Ency. of McCoy Pottery, Huxford $19.95
3313 Collector's Ency. of Niloak, Gifford $19.95
1039 Collector's Ency. of Nippon Porcelain I, Van Patten ..$19.95
2089 Collector's Ency. of Nippon Porcelain II, Van Patten $24.95
1665 Collector's Ency. of Nippon Porcelain III, Van Patten $24.95
1034 Collector's Ency. of Roseville Pottery, Huxford $19.95
1035 Collector's Ency. of Roseville Pottery, 2nd Ed., Huxford $19.95
3314 Collector's Ency. of Van Briggle Art Pottery, Sasicki ..$24.95
2339 Collector's Guide to Shawnee Pottery, Vanderbilt $19.95
1425 Cookie Jars, Westfall $9.95
2275 Czechoslovakian Glass & Collectibles, Barta $16.95
3315 Elegant Glassware of the Depression Era, 5th Ed., Florence ..$19.95
3318 Glass Animals of the Depression Era, Garmon & Spencer $19.95
2024 Kitchen Glassware of the Depression Years, 4th Ed.,Florence $19.95
2379 Lehner's Ency. of U.S. Marks on Pottery, Porcelain & Clay $24.95
2394 Oil Lamps II, Thuro $24.95
3322 Pocket Guide to Depression Glass, 8th Ed., Florence ..$9.95
2345 Portland Glass, Ladd $24.95
1670 Red Wing Collectibles, DePasquale $9.95
1440 Red Wing Stoneware, DePasquale $9.95
1958 So. Potteries Blue Ridge Dinnerware, 3rd Ed., Newbound . $14.95
2221 Standard Carnival Glass, 3rd Ed., Edwards.................$24.95
1848 Very Rare Glassware of the Depression Years, Florence $24.95
2140 Very Rare Glassware of the Depression Years, Second Series . $24.95
3326 Very Rare Glassware of the Depression Era, Third Series $24.95
3327 Watt Pottery - Identification & Value Guide, Morris $19.95
2224 World of Salt Shakers, 2nd Ed., Lechner $24.95

BOOKS ON DOLLS & TOYS

2079 Barbie Fashion, Vol. 1, 1959-1967, Eames $24.95
3310 Black Dolls - 1820-1990 - Id. & Value Guide, Perkins .$17.95
1514 Character Toys & Collectibles 1st Series, Longest $19.95
1750 Character Toys & Collectibles, 2nd Series, Longest ...$19.95
1529 Collector's Ency. of Barbie Dolls, DeWein $19.95
2338 Collector's Ency. of Disneyana, Longest & Stern $24.95
2342 Madame Alexander Price Guide #17, Smith $9.95
1540 Modern Toys, 1930-1980, Baker $19.95
2343 Patricia Smith's Doll Values Antique to Modern, 8th ed $12.95
1886 Stern's Guide to Disney $14.95

2139 Stern's Guide to Disney, 2nd Series $14.95
1513 Teddy Bears & Steiff Animals, Mandel $9.95
1817 Teddy Bears & Steiff Animals, 2nd, Mandel................$19.95
2084 Teddy Bears, Annalees & Steiff Animals, 3rd, Mandel $19.95
2028 Toys, Antique & Collectible, Longest $14.95
1808 Wonder of Barbie, Manos.....................................$9.95
1430 World of Barbie Dolls, Manos $9.95

OTHER COLLECTIBLES

1457 American Oak Furniture, McNerney $9.95
2269 Antique Brass & Copper, Gaston $16.95
2333 Antique & Collectible Marbles, Grist, 3rd Ed. $9.95
1712 Antique & Collectible Thimbles, Mathis $19.95
1748 Antique Purses, Holiner $19.95
1868 Antique Tools, Our American Heritage, McNerney $9.95
1426 Arrowheads & Projectile Points, Hothem $7.95
1278 Art Nouveau & Art Deco Jewelry, Baker $9.95
1714 Black Collectibles, Gibbs $19.95
1128 Bottle Pricing Guide, 3rd Ed., Cleveland $7.95
1751 Christmas Collectibles, Whitmyer $19.95
1752 Christmas Ornaments, Johnston $19.95
2132 Collector's Ency. of American Furniture, Vol. I, Swedberg .$24.95
2271 Collector's Ency. of American Furniture, Vol. II, Swedberg $24.95
2338 Collector's Ency. of Disneyana, Longest & Stern $24.95
2018 Collector's Ency. of Graniteware, Greguire $24.95
2083 Collector's Ency. of Russel Wright Designs, Kerr........$19.95
2337 Collector's Guide to Decoys, Book II, Huxford $16.95
2340 Collector's Guide to Easter Collectibles, Burnett $16.95
1441 Collector's Guide to Post Cards, Wood $9.95
2276 Decoys, Kangas $24.95
1629 Doorstops, Id. & Values, Betoria $9.95
1716 Fifty Years of Fashion Jewelry, Baker $19.95
3316 Flea Market Trader, 8th Ed., Huxford........................$9.95
3317 Florence's Standard Baseball Card Price Gd., 5th Ed. .$9.95
1755 Furniture of the Depression Era, Swedberg $19.95
2278 Grist's Machine Made & Contemporary Marbles $9.95
1424 Hatpins & Hatpin Holders, Baker $9.95
3319 Huxford's Collectible Advertising - Id. & Value Gd. $17.95
1181 100 Years of Collectible Jewelry, Baker $9.95
2023 Keen Kutter Collectibles, 2nd Ed., Heuring $14.95
2216 Kitchen Antiques - 1790–1940, McNerney $14.95
3320 Modern Guns - Id. & Val. Gd., 9th Ed., Quertermous $12.95
1965 Pine Furniture, Our Am. Heritage, McNerney $14.95
3321 Ornamental & Figural Nutcrackers, Rittenhouse $16.95
2026 Railroad Collectibles, 4th Ed., Baker $14.95
1632 Salt & Pepper Shakers, Guarnaccia $9.95
1888 Salt & Pepper Shakers II, Guarnaccia $14.95
2220 Salt & Pepper Shakers III, Guarnaccia $14.95
3323 Schroeder's Antique Price Guide, 11th Ed. $12.95
3324 Schroeder's Antique & Coll. 1993 Engag. Calendar.....$9.95
2346 Sheet Music Ref. & Price Guide, Patik & Guiheen $18.95
2096 Silverplated Flatware, 4th Ed., Hagan $14.95
3325 Standard Knife Collector's Guide, Stewart $12.95
2348 20th Century Fashionable Plastic Jewelry, Baker $19.95
2349 Value Guide to Baseball Collectibles, Raycraft..........$16.95

Schroeder's ANTIQUES Price Guide

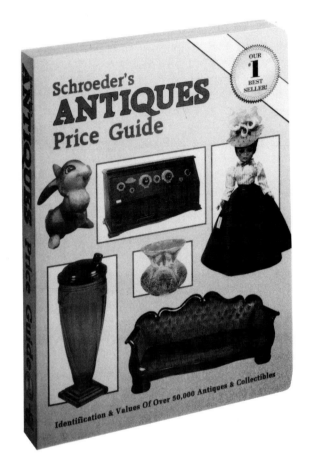

Schroeder's Antiques Price Guide is the #1 best-selling antiques & collectibles value guide on the market today, and here's why . . . More than 300 authors, well-known dealers, and top-notch collectors work together with our editors to bring you accurate information regarding pricing and identification. More than 45,000 items in almost 500 categories are listed along with hundreds of sharp original photos that illustrate not only the rare and unusual, but the common, popular collectibles as well. Each large close-up shot shows important details clearly. Every subject is represented with histories and background information, a feature not found in any of our competitors' publications. Our editors keep abreast of newly-developing trends, often adding several new categories a year as the need arises. If it merits the interest of today's collector, you'll find it in Schroeder's. And you can feel confident that the information we publish is up to date and accurate. Our advisors thoroughly check each category to spot inconsistencies, listings that may not be entirely reflective of market dealings, and lines too vague to be of merit. Only the best of the lot remains for publication. Without doubt, you'll find Schroeder's Antiques Price Guide the only one to buy for reliable information and values.

8½ x 11", 608 Pages   **$12.95**

COLLECTOR BOOKS

A Division of Schroeder Publishing Co., Inc.